quick-fix
indian

Also by Ruta Kahate

5 Spices, 50 Dishes

Easy, Exotic
Dishes in

**30 minutes
or less**

quick-fix
indian

ruta kahate

**Andrews McMeel
Publishing, LLC**
Kansas City · Sydney · London

Andrews McMeel Publishing, LLC
an Andrews McMeel Universal company
1130 Walnut Street, Kansas City, Missouri 64106

12 13 14 15 16 RR2 10 9 8 7 6 5 4 3 2 1

ISBN: 978-1-4494-0977-7
Library of Congress Control Number: 2011932639

Photos by Ben Pieper, p. 52, 79; all other photos courtesy of iStockphoto.com

www.andrewsmcmeel.com
www.ruta.in

ATTENTION: SCHOOLS AND BUSINESSES
Andrews McMeel books are available at quantity discounts with bulk purchase for educational, business, or sales promotional use. For information, please e-mail the Andrews McMeel Publishing Special Sales Department:
specialsales@amuniversal.com

This book is for my two little girls,
Mira and Lola, who robbed me
of all my free time and made
me a quick-fix cook.

You make my life sing.
You fill my already busy days
with sparkle and fireworks,
always keeping me on
my toes—and I wouldn't
have it any other way.

contents

acknowledgments   ix

introduction   xi

quick-fix indian pantry   3

shortcut shelf   11

chapter 1
brisk breakfasts   23

chapter 2
lightning lunches   37

chapter 3
swift soups   53

chapter 4
speedy salads and raitas   65

chapter 5
mains in minutes   79

chapter 6
express veggies   99

chapter 7
snappy staples   113

chapter 8
curries in a hurry (dals, too)   129

chapter 9
rapid relishes   149

chapter 10
zippy snacks   159

chapter 11
double-quick desserts   171

chapter 12
last-minute libations   185

metric conversions and equivalents   199

index   202

acknowledgments

Writing a cookbook is a lot like working in a restaurant kitchen. No matter how skilled the chef, success ultimately depends on a highly synchronized team effort.

I'm deeply grateful to my own *Quick-Fix Indian* team of professionals:

Andrews McMeel, my publisher—for having a *Quick-Fix* series in the first place; it's a perfect match for the way I cook right now.

Carole Bidnick, my superagent—for introducing me to Andrews McMeel; her professionalism and energy are inspiring.

Jean Lucas, my editor—for being so supportive and accommodating while still keeping everything on track.

The art department at Andrews McMeel—for their gorgeous design and infinite patience with my nit-picking.

Tammie Barker, my enthusiastic publicist—for her constant and infectious good cheer.

My recipe testers—for making time to cook from my recipes and document the results despite being busy professionals.

And finally, Neville Desouza, my husband and friend—for putting aside his own work time and again to critique my manuscript. Everyone should be so lucky to have an advertising pro at home.

Thank you all. I had great fun writing this book!

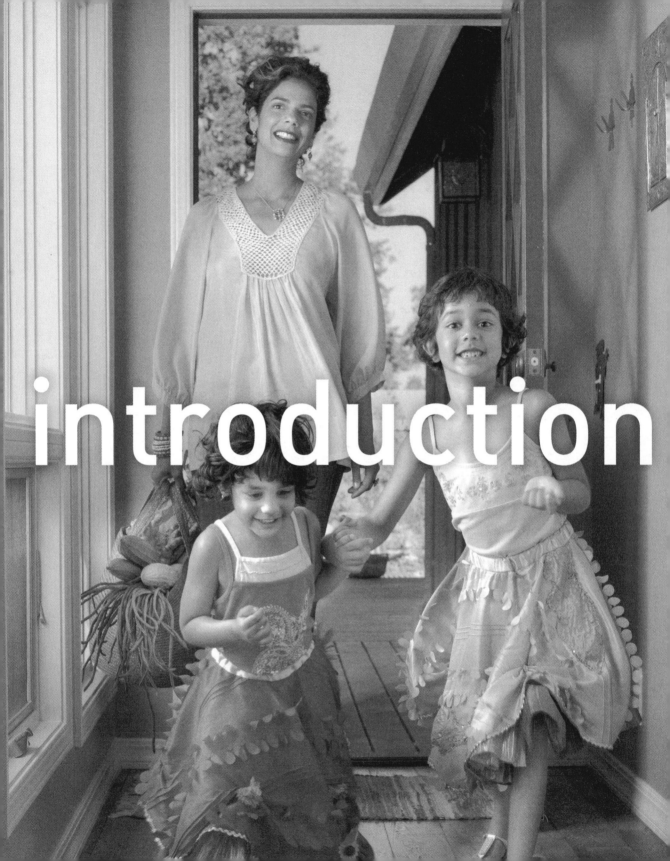

introduction

how i quick-fixed myself

For several years, I ran a cooking school in Oakland, California. My intention was to demystify Indian food; to demonstrate that, contrary to popular belief, this exotic cuisine could in fact be simple to cook at home. But *simple* can be a subjective term. As my early students will testify (while rolling their eyes), I'd have them make everything from scratch—grind every whole spice and blend every masala fresh for each recipe. The results were superb, I reasoned, so why do it any other way?

Why, indeed. I found the answer when my little daughters, Mira and Lola, came along, bringing with them the million and one chores that weigh down a parent's already busy schedule. Suddenly, simple had to get a whole lot simpler. I discovered smart shortcuts, convenient techniques, and quick-cooking ingredients that didn't compromise on taste or nutrition. I applied a lot of those ideas to my school, much to my students' delight. Several of them were overextended parents or busy executives who loved to cook but couldn't spare hours to source and prep a menu.

Sounds like you? If so, you'll like this book; it reflects the way I like to cook and eat today. Using your Quick-Fix Indian Pantry and Shortcut Shelf, you, too, will be able to create quick dishes that are fresh, nutritious, and, dare I say, exotic.

how to use this book

I'll let you in on a little secret. I don't actually plan my weekly menus; I'm too seat-of-the-pants for that. Instead I keep my Quick-Fix Indian Pantry and Shortcut Shelf always stocked so I'm free to respond to the moment—shrimp fresh enough to jump into my basket, a glut of organic strawberries, the unexpected dinner guest, the head cold that I feel coming on. In short, spontaneity is great, but only if you're well organized.

So the first thing to do is to take this book shopping and stock your Quick-Fix Indian Pantry. Next, tackle your Shortcut Shelf: the recurring homemade items you'll always be reaching for. And then get cooking.

Here's the very best part: Every one of these recipes has been designed so you can make the dish—from start to finish—in 30 minutes or less. That includes any soaking or marinating time. If you decide to soak or marinate longer, great; but it's not necessary for the success of the dish.

Of course, I'm assuming you're comfortable in the kitchen and you have basic cooking skills. If you've never chopped an onion before, you may need to add a few minutes to the total time, depending on the recipe. The good news is, even if you're a total novice, you'll be able to make these dishes without being overwhelmed.

The recipes themselves are from all over the subcontinent, where I've spent half my life cooking and eating. If you notice several dishes from the tiny state of Goa, that's where I'm spending a lot of time these days. This coastal paradise is unique in India, both for its laid-back lifestyle and its remarkable cuisine.

The structure of this book is slightly unusual; in addition to the usual courses I've added two sections: Breakfast and Lunch. Since most people aren't familiar with the Indian versions of those meals, I thought it would be nice to give you some quick options such as Breakfast Chana Masala (page 33), or Grilled Paneer and Beet Salad (page 41) for a light lunch.

As for special equipment, there are just three things you'll need: a blender to make your soups and wet masalas; a good electric coffee grinder that you'll strictly use for grinding spices; and a small, sturdy mortar and pestle, which is better for grinding tiny amounts— the seeds of just one cardamom pod, for instance. You can even put the little ones to work; my girls love sitting on the floor and pounding spices. It gets the job done and keeps them out of trouble.

By the way, cooking is all about touch and feel. There's simply no way to predict exactly how long to cook a potato in order to make it tender enough to mash. One crop may be different from another, your gas burner may not be as strong as mine, your kitchen may be at a higher altitude—nature doesn't always cooperate with a well-written recipe. So, to repeat what I used to tell my students, "you just have to cook it until it's done." While I assure you that all these recipes can be made in under 30 minutes, I've refrained from specifying exact timings for every single step—because I believe you'll get better results by feeling your way through the process instead of constantly watching the clock. Just read the entire recipe through before you begin; that way there are no surprises.

Finally, rather than over-intellectualizing cooking, I follow this mantra: *If it tastes good, it'll get eaten.* It's as simple as that. To me, there really is no bigger joy than cooking up a meal, then watching it all disappear. And making tasty meals in these not-so-relaxed times is all about being prepared. So get organized and watch those plates being wiped clean.

Cook and be happy!

quick-fix
indian

quick-fix
indian
pantry

shopping list

Depending on where you live, most of these ingredients should be available at your local supermarket. Whatever you can't find should be available at a health food store or Indian grocery.

When you have a little more time to curl up with this cookbook, turn the page for the backstory on the spices and other ingredients you've bought.

spices

Buy small amounts to ensure freshness. Whenever possible, buy whole spices and grind to order; powdered spices quickly lose flavor. Two exceptions: It's okay to buy ground turmeric and cayenne. The first five spices are the ones that you'll use the most in the recipes in this book.

- Cayenne
- Coriander seeds
- Cumin seeds
- Ground turmeric
- Mustard seeds
- Black peppercorns
- Cinnamon sticks
- Dried red chile peppers
- Fennel seeds
- Fenugreek seeds (health food/Indian store)
- Green cardamom pods
- Indian bay leaves (health food/Indian store)
- Nutmeg
- Saffron threads
- Whole cloves

canola oil

canned goods

Garbanzos (chickpeas), red beans, black beans, black-eyed peas
Peeled and chopped tomatoes, tomato puree
Coconut milk. Avoid the nonfat kind; it's thin and flavorless. I like Chaokoh brand.
Water-packed tuna

basmati and medium-grain rice

flours

- All-purpose flour
- Chickpea flour (also known as chana besan or gram flour)
- Cream of wheat/farina (also known as *rava* or *sooji*). If necessary, substitute semolina.
- White whole wheat flour. If necessary, substitute regular whole wheat flour.

dals

- Green mung beans
- Whole lentils. Buy any of the following: brown, petite dark brown (*masoor dal*), green, or speckled blue-green Le Puy lentils.
- Split lentils (pink in color, also known as masoor dal)
- *Chana dal* (skinned and split Indian chickpeas)

seeds and nuts
- Brown or "natural" poppy seeds. Avoid the blue-black variety.
- Sesame seeds
- Whole, unsalted—preferably untoasted—peanuts, cashews, almonds, and pistachios. Store in the fridge.

dried, shredded, unsweetened coconut
- Avoid the sweetened variety, such as used for angel food cake.

freezer
- Peeled shrimp
- Beef top sirloin
- Boneless chicken breasts
- Peas
- Spinach
- Okra

fridge
- Unsalted butter (to make ghee)
- Plain yogurt
- Tortillas or pita bread
- Fresh eggs

produce
- Fresh ginger
- Fresh garlic
- Fresh cilantro
- Serrano chiles
- Fresh curry leaves (health food/Indian store)
- Yellow and red onions
- Russet and Yukon Gold potatoes
- Tomatoes
- All other produce, according to need

shopping list demystified

spices

These building blocks of Indian flavor are also valued for their therapeutic properties. While Indian cooking may use hundreds of different spices, we'll keep things simple with a few key spices that are commonly available.

Cayenne: This potent red powder is made by grinding dried cayenne peppers, a variety that's as hot as the Tabasco pepper. Note that the actual heat of ground cayenne may vary quite a bit, depending on where and when the chiles were cultivated, so you may want to adjust the quantity in the recipes to suit your comfort level. The compound capsaicin, responsible for the heat in cayenne, has strong anti-inflammatory properties and is widely used in pain medication.

Coriander seeds: These dried, ocher-colored seeds (technically fruits) of the cilantro herb have a nutty, lemony flavor that's very different from that of the herb. In India, coriander seeds are widely used, mostly in their powdered form. I use this spice often enough that I grind ¼ cup of seeds every week after lightly toasting them on a hot skillet.

Cumin seeds: Cumin is one of the key spices in Indian cooking. It's used in all kinds of masalas, including garam masala and Madras curry powder. It's mixed into *raitas* and brewed into hot teas, due to its digestive properties. The seeds are used whole and powdered; I grind and bottle a small quantity of cumin seeds every week. Note that Westerners often confuse cumin with caraway, which comes from the same family; while they look similar, they taste very different.

Ground turmeric: An earthy-tasting member of the ginger family, turmeric has been used in India for centuries as a spice—and a medicine. Today, turmeric's active compound curcumin (responsible for the dried spice's bright yellow color) is being widely studied for its anti-oxidant properties and its ability to arrest some cancers and improve brain function. Some scientists are even connecting the dots between high turmeric usage and the low rate of Alzheimer's in India.

Mustard seeds: These tiny, mildly bitter seeds play a big role in Indian cooking. In their whole form, they're fried until they pop, transferring their flavor to the oil—and in turn, to the dish being cooked. Mustard seeds are also ground to lend their characteristic pungency to a dish or pickle. My recipes use the black-brown seeds, but if you can't find them, go ahead and use the more commonly available yellow ones.

Black peppercorns: Native to India's Malabar Coast, pepper berries grow on vines and are picked while unripe, then sun-dried until black and wrinkly. Peppercorns were the main source of heat in Indian cooking before the chile pepper was introduced five centuries ago. Back then, black pepper was worth more than gold; the search for new trade routes to this precious spice led Christopher Columbus to (inadvertently) discover America.

Cinnamon sticks: In India, the dried inner bark of the cinnamon tree is used in savory dishes rather than in sweets. Cinnamon is a potent spice, rich in essential oils; a small piece can transform an entire dish. True cinnamon is native to Sri Lanka, and most of the world's supply still comes from that tiny nation. Here in the United States, what's labeled as cinnamon or Chinese cinnamon is more likely to be the bark of the cassia tree, a related species with similar, although less delicate, flavor.

Dried red chile peppers: Indispensable to Indian food today, the chile pepper was actually introduced to India as recently as the sixteenth century, brought by Portuguese sailors from the New World. Today, hundreds of varieties are grown in India, from the long red Kashmiri chile that imparts more color than heat, to the incendiary Bhut Jolokia, one of the hottest in the world. When handling dried chile peppers, break off the stem end and shake out the seeds. Don't forget to wash your hands afterward; the oils can irritate your skin and eyes.

Fennel seeds: Related to cumin and caraway, the fennel seed has a sweet, licorice taste with a nice bite to it. In India, fennel seeds aren't just used for cooking; they're also eaten raw or candied, as a mouth freshener or digestive after the meal (which explains that plate of vividly colored seeds that arrives with your check at your local Indian restaurant).

Fenugreek seeds: Brown and slightly bitter, the tiny fenugreek seed lends its flavor to everything from Madras curry powder to generic maple syrup. The seeds are also soaked to grow fenugreek sprouts, a favorite herb in India. Interesting factoid: In a recent Australian clinical study, fenugreek increased libido in male subjects by 25 percent or more. Didn't I say spices are good for you?

Green cardamom pods: Green cardamom is regarded as the queen of spices in India, where it grows on the slopes of the Cardamom Hills in the south of the country. One of the most expensive spices by weight, cardamom is very aromatic, so just a little works wonders in savory and sweet dishes. The pods are even chewed after meals as a breath freshener and digestive. Buy only whole cardamom pods; the exposed or ground seeds will lose their flavor quickly.

Indian bay leaves: The name is misleading; these dried leaves come from an entirely different tree than the Bay Laurel. The so-called Indian bay leaf tastes a bit like cinnamon, only milder. It's much longer than its Western counterpart, with three veins along the length of the leaf instead of one.

Nutmeg: This spice used to be priceless a few centuries ago, since the nutmeg tree grew in only one place in the entire world: the tiny Banda Islands in Indonesia. Today, ground nutmeg is easily found in your local supermarket. If available, buy the inch-long nutmeg seed instead—unlike the ground version, the seed will keep for a long time without losing flavor, and you can grate it as needed with a Microplane or fine grater.

Saffron threads: If cardamom is the queen of spices, saffron is the undisputed king. It takes several thousand hand-picked saffron crocus flowers to make a single ounce of dried saffron threads—which explains why it's the world's most expensive spice. Fortunately, a little saffron goes a long way; heating a few threads quickly releases an abundance of fragrance and a brilliant golden hue.

Cloves: These are actually dried flower buds of the clove tree. Cloves are an intense flavoring agent; they pack quite a bit of "sweet heat." So be sure to pick them out of the finished dish once they've done their work. Aside from their whole form, cloves are also ground for use in masalas. And like cardamom pods, they're chewed after meals as a breath freshener and digestive.

Tip: Indian bay leaves and fenugreek seeds (*tejpatta* and *methi dana* in Hindi) are two ingredients that may be hard to find at your local supermarket. They may be available at a health food store; you'll definitely get them at an Indian grocery store. But don't go crazy; this is a quick-fix cookbook, after all. If necessary, omit both ingredients and carry on with the recipe.

salt

I don't like prescribing amounts for salt because everyone's tolerance for salt is different. Besides, there are so many varieties out there with varying degrees of saltiness. I use kosher salt in most of my cooking. For certain things—shrimp comes to mind—sea salt seems to bring out the best flavor. You yourself may use table salt. So do please use your own judgment—if you're a real beginner, start with a ¼ teaspoon and then adjust according to your personal taste. I will tell you this: Don't be afraid of salt. While moderation is a good thing, it's a total waste to make a great dish and then eat it undersalted.

oils

When you're getting started with Indian cooking, there's no better oil than canola. Low in saturated fat, it has no flavor of its own. Other oils used in India, such as coconut, peanut, unrefined mustard, and untoasted sesame, all have strong flavors— you need a bit of practice to know where to use them so they won't clash with your dish. For those of you who'd like to take this a step further, I've included suggestions for an appropriate alternative oil in some of the recipes.

basmati and medium-grain rice

Indians generally save Basmati for special dishes like pilafs and *biryani*, preferring a robust medium-grain rice for daily use. Note that while good medium-grain rice is easy to find, a lot of what passes for Basmati these days seems to lack flavor. My advice: Buy small amounts and let your nose be the judge—look for a mild floral aroma.

flours

All-purpose flour: I'm sure you already have this in your pantry. It's one of the most versatile flours, used in everything from cakes and cookies to poories.

Chickpea flour: Made from ground chickpeas, this flour is high in protein and gluten-free. Also called *besan* or gram flour.

Cream of wheat/farina: This is a coarse flour milled from soft wheat. If you can't find it anywhere, you may substitute semolina, which is made from the harder durum wheat. Also called *rava* or *sooji*.

Whole wheat flour: While you can use regular whole wheat flour, the newer white whole wheat flour is much better for Indian breads, since it's milled from a type of wheat very similar to the Indian variety.

dals

While there are a multitude of pulses that go by the name dal, we'll use only four kinds in our recipes: green mung beans, whole lentils, split lentils, and *chana dal*.

Green mung beans: Native to the Indian subcontinent, where they've been cultivated for four millennia. Packed with protein, they're one of the most common dals in Indian cooking. The split mung bean is called *mung dal*.

Whole lentils: These look like tiny, little lenses, which is how they got their name. Buy any of the following: brown, petite dark brown (*masoor dal*), green, or the speckled blue-green lentils from Le Puy, France.

Split lentils: Pink in color; they're basically brown lentils (masoor dal) that have been skinned and split, revealing the pinkish interior.

Chana dal: Resembling little yellow disks, this dal is the skinned and split version of the Indian chickpea.

herbs and chiles

Fresh cilantro: If this herb shows up in a lot of my recipes, that's because it's a favorite ingredient in Indian cooking. I realize there are a few people who have an aversion to cilantro; if you're one of them, feel free to leave it out.

Serrano chiles: I use these green peppers for a couple of reasons. They work really well in my cooking, and they're widely available. Buy small quantities and store in the crisper section of your refrigerator.

Fresh curry leaves: There's really no substitute for curry leaves, so simply omit them if you can't find any. If they are available, buy a bunch; the fresh leaves will last for a few weeks in your refrigerator if stored properly. Without wetting, wrap the leaves in layers of paper towels and place in a resealable plastic bag in the crisper section. Do not freeze. And don't bother with dried curry leaves—they taste like sawdust.

With a well-stocked Indian pantry and fridge, you'll always be ready to cook—for yourself, your family, or the whole soccer team.

shortcut
shelf

Ghee   13

Garlic Paste   14

Ginger Paste   15

Red Masala   16

Green Masala   17

Garam Masala   18

Brown Onions   19

Paneer   20

If you've bought your spices and the ingredients for your Quick-Fix Indian Pantry, it's time to put together your Shortcut Shelf. Here you'll keep the "usual suspects" of Indian cooking: masalas (spice blends), brown onions, ginger and garlic pastes—a grand total of eight essential, recurring items. A fair number of recipes in this cookbook call for one or more of them, so they're really convenient and time-saving to have on hand.

Your Shortcut Shelf is also a fantastic resource for impromptu creativity. Let's say you pull out a pork chop for dinner. If you've got a batch of red masala in the fridge, you may find yourself rubbing a tablespoon on the chop before tossing it on the grill. Or adding a handful of brown onions to transform your next batch of mashed potatoes. Or stirring in a smidgen of garlic paste while whipping up a quick morning scramble—a step you'd probably skip if you had to peel a clove of garlic. Since almost everything on the Shortcut Shelf is pure, concentrated flavor, the possibilities are endless.

A note to all the procrastinators out there: If you don't have the time or inclination to put together your Shortcut Shelf, relax. In most cases, you can make these items to order and still have your recipe ready within 30 minutes. But over time, you'll find that having these essentials on hand makes a lot of sense.

ghee

makes 1 pound

Ghee is clarified butter with a nuttier taste. While both are made by heating butter to separate the milk solids from the butterfat, there's an additional step for ghee: You continue cooking the butterfat until the milk solids caramelize, giving the ghee its distinctive flavor. In India, ghee is prized as the finest cooking medium. Also, to enjoy its aromatic flavor, it's spread on flatbread, poured over rice, or even just served alongside the meal. And apparently, ghee isn't just loved by mere mortals; since ancient times, it's been called the "food of the Devas (gods)." Even today, it's the primary offering in the sacred fire during any Hindu ritual.

1 pound unsalted butter; I like Plugrá best for its high fat content

Melt the butter in a heavy-bottomed pan over low heat—that's it. Okay, maybe there's a bit more to it than that.

The butter will go through a few stages before it clarifies. First, it will melt and begin to foam on top. (You may skim this foam off if you like; I never do.) Next, as the moisture in the fat begins to evaporate, the foam will give way to milk solids that eventually settle to the bottom of the pan. The butter has clarified.

Now you're looking for color. I like ghee that looks like molten gold—this happens when the milk solids at the bottom of the pan have turned a dark brown. Watch it carefully at this stage because it can easily burn. As soon as the ghee reaches the exact hue you're looking for, immediately take it off the heat and set it aside in a cool place for 5 minutes.

Line a tea strainer with a double thickness of cheesecloth or even a square of paper towel. Decant the ghee through this strainer *slowly,* trying not to disturb the milk solids.

This whole process takes about 20 minutes from start to finish.

Ghee usually achieves a soft, semisolid state once it cools to room temperature. This is the perfect consistency for stir-frying veggies, frying an omelet, or stirring into soups as a special garnish. But my recipes all call for melted ghee because it's just easier to measure.

Tip

Although ghee will keep at room temperature for a month, here's what I recommend: When you make a batch, keep most of it in a tightly covered jar in the refrigerator and a small quantity near your range, replenishing as required. Once you've made your own ghee, I'm positive you'll never go back to the store-bought kind.

garlic paste

makes ½ cup

Garlic and ginger are used in so many Indian recipes (often together) that it's a huge time-saver to have premade pastes on hand. These days, it's getting easier to find them commercially, so if your supermarket or health food store has a quality brand of garlic paste, by all means buy a bottle.

Otherwise, follow the instructions below. Just remember these rules: Garlic paste should never be stored at room temperature. Store in the refrigerator for a maximum of 2 weeks (write the expiry date on the jar) to prevent bacteria from forming. Commercial pastes have some type of acid (usually citric) to prevent this, so they keep for up to 3 months in the fridge.

4 ounces garlic cloves, peeled
1 tablespoon canola oil
2 tablespoons water

Place the garlic cloves in a blender jar. With the motor running, first add the oil and then the water. Blend until you get a smooth paste, scraping down the sides often. Transfer to a clean glass jar, cover, and refrigerate immediately.

Tips

In a pinch, you can use a zester or Japanese grater to make a small quantity of garlic paste to order.

Every once in a while, garlic paste may turn bright green in the fridge. There are various theories on why this happens, but rest assured, it's quite normal and has no effect on safety or flavor. If it bothers you, make a fresh batch.

ginger paste

makes ½ cup

As I mentioned in the previous recipe, if you can find a good brand of ginger paste commercially, go ahead and buy a bottle.

If store-bought isn't an option, follow the recipe below. And don't forget these rules: Homemade ginger paste should never be stored at room temperature. Store in the refrigerator for a maximum of 2 weeks (write the expiry date on the jar) to prevent bacteria from forming. Commercial ginger pastes usually contain citric acid to prevent this, so they keep for up to 3 months in the fridge.

4 ounces fresh ginger, peeled and
    coarsely chopped
2 tablespoons canola oil
3 tablespoons water

Place the ginger in a blender jar. With the motor running, first add the oil and then the water. Blend until you get a smooth paste, scraping down the sides often. Transfer to a clean, glass jar, cover, and refrigerate immediately.

Tip

You can use the zester attachment on your Microplane to finely grate ginger to order, then substitute for ginger paste in the recipe.

red masala

makes ¼ cup

The word *masala* colloquially refers to a mixture or blend of different things. For instance, a Bollywood film that covers multiple genres—romance, action, and tragedy—would be called a "masala movie." In culinary terms, a masala is either a dry blend of spices or a wet blend such as red masala, where spices are combined with other ingredients and then ground to a fine paste.

This masala gets its crimson color from the paprika, but most of the heat comes from the cayenne. I like the 1:1 ratio of these powdered chiles, but if you want to reduce the heat, just increase the paprika and proportionately decrease the cayenne.

¼ teaspoon cumin seeds
14 whole cloves
10 black peppercorns
1 (2-inch) stick cinnamon
1 tablespoon cayenne
1 tablespoon paprika

½ teaspoon ground turmeric
2 teaspoons Ginger Paste (page 15)
2 teaspoons Garlic Paste (page 14)
2 tablespoons apple cider vinegar
1 teaspoon granulated sugar

Using a clean spice grinder, grind the cumin, cloves, peppercorns, and cinnamon to a fine powder. Transfer to a small bowl and stir in the cayenne, paprika, and turmeric. Add the ginger paste, garlic paste, vinegar, and sugar and mix into a smooth paste.

Store in an airtight glass bottle in the refrigerator for up to 1 month.

Tip

Just because the same masala goes into several recipes, it doesn't mean they'll end up tasting the same. Quite the contrary; in some dishes the masala dominates; in others, it's barely there in the background.

green masala

makes a little more than ½ cup

Unlike the similar-colored pastes used in Thai cooking, my green and red masalas aren't just for curries. We'll also use them in other interesting ways—such as stuffing green masala into okra (page 101) and making a sauce for baby potatoes (page 96). After you're familiar with all the ways I use masalas in this cookbook, I'm sure you'll begin experimenting with them, too.

Here we combine spices with cilantro and green chiles to create a wet masala that's very bright, both in flavor and color.

1 teaspoon cumin seeds
1 heaping teaspoon coriander seeds
6 whole cloves
1½ cups tightly packed chopped
  fresh cilantro
2 small serrano chiles, coarsely chopped

1 teaspoon Garlic Paste (page 14)
1 teaspoon Ginger Paste (page 15)
½ teaspoon ground turmeric
½ teaspoon granulated sugar
3 tablespoons freshly squeezed lemon juice
Up to ¼ cup water

Using a clean spice grinder, finely grind the cumin, coriander, and cloves together. Then place all the ingredients except the water in a blender jar. Turn on the blender and—with the motor running—add the water to blend to a fine puree. Use only as much water as required to make a smooth, fine paste.

Store in an airtight glass bottle in the refrigerator for up to 1 month.

garam masala

makes about ¼ cup

Made with dry-roasted spices and a pinch of salt, this is a classic "dry" masala, unlike the previous two "wet" ones. *Garam* means "hot"; but this masala yields a very different heat than the kind you get from chiles; here it's from the intensity of the spices.

In India, there are thousands of recipes for garam masala—and they all taste different! This particular recipe is my own; the spice blend has been tailored for the dishes in this cookbook. A store-bought garam masala could change the way these dishes are supposed to taste, even overpower them.

2 teaspoons cumin seeds
2 tablespoons coriander seeds
5 whole green cardamom pods
½ teaspoon black peppercorns

8 whole cloves
½ teaspoon fennel seeds
1 (2-inch) stick cinnamon
Pinch of salt

Roast each spice separately on a heavy, dry skillet until lightly browned and fragrant. (Roasting spices intensifies their flavor while drying out the seeds so they grind easily.) Peel the green cardamom; reserve the seeds for the masala and discard the pods. Using a clean spice grinder, powder all the garam masala ingredients together until fine.

Store in an airtight glass bottle for up to 1 month.

Tip

The amount this recipe yields should last you at least a month, after which the masala will lose its potency. So make just one recipe at a time; it takes barely 10 minutes.

brown onions

makes 2 cups

These are very dark brown onions—just a step before they get burned. (I actually called them Burnt Onions in my first cookbook, *5 Spices, 50 Dishes*.) These onions are a magical ingredient, darkening my Andhra Chicken Curry to just the right rich color (page 131), or doing double duty as flavor-booster-and-garnish in my "Instant" Chicken Biryani (page 126). Home cooks in South India fry these aromatic onions in large quantities, browning them until they're dry and crisp before draining and bottling.

Once you have a batch of brown onions on your Shortcut Shelf, you'll discover how versatile they are. You can sprinkle them in a salad of avocado, cherry tomatoes, and romaine lettuce. Or garnish a curried pumpkin soup. Or serve a big pile alongside your steak and mashed potatoes.

2 medium yellow onions
½ cup canola oil

Halve each onion from stem to tip, then thinly slice into half-moons. Separate into individual slices using your fingers.

In the largest skillet you own, heat the oil on high until it starts rippling.

Add the onion slices and stir until they're all coated with oil. Spread out evenly in a thin layer. Now leave the skillet on high heat and wait; I know you'll feel the urge to keep stirring, but control it! We want to end up with crisp, dark brown onions, not a mushy mess.

The slices on the periphery will start to brown first; stir them into the center of the pan. Once again, spread everything out in a thin layer. Keep doing this until *all* the onion slices begin to color.

When they're all lightly colored, set the heat to medium-low and let them cook. Stir only occasionally, remembering to spread them out evenly. This is when the slices will start losing their moisture, turning dark brown and crisp without actually getting burned.

When evenly browned and crisp, drain on paper towels. They will crisp further as they cool.

Store in an airtight glass bottle in the refrigerator for up to 1 month.

Tip

It takes a bit of practice to make perfect brown onions, but you'll get the hang of it in no time.

paneer

makes 2 pounds

Paneer is a fresh farmer cheese widely used by North Indian vegetarians as a protein. The cheese itself is 100 percent vegetarian, as it uses lemon juice or vinegar instead of rennet as a coagulating agent. If you have a good source for fresh paneer, fine. If not, making your own paneer is as simple as curdling milk. By the way, this is one Shortcut Shelf ingredient I'd ask you to prepare only when you know you're going to make a paneer dish sometime that week.

1½ gallons whole or low-fat milk
½ cup freshly squeezed lemon juice or white
   vinegar (more if needed)

Bring the milk to a boil in a heavy-bottomed saucepan. Stir occasionally so a skin doesn't form on the surface. When the milk begins to rise, add the lemon juice while stirring constantly. The milk will instantly curdle and the whey will separate.

Line a sieve with a large piece of cheesecloth and strain the liquid through it. Lift the four corners of the cloth and tie the ends to make a small bundle. Place the sieve over a bowl to drain out all the remaining whey; this will take about an hour.

To make a block of paneer, you'll need to press the drained curds under a weight. Place the cheesecloth bundle on a cutting board. Place another board on top and place a heavy weight on it. (A large pot filled with water will do nicely.) In less than an hour, you'll have your very own, homemade paneer.

Tip

Paneer is a fresh, unripened cheese, so make sure you consume it within 3 days of preparation.

brisk breakfasts

Spicy Coastal Scramble   25

Egg Roll   26

Eggless Omelet   27

Gobi Flatbread   28

Indian Grits with Vegetables   30

Kids' Favorite Banana Fritters   31

Comforting Rice and Yogurt   32

Breakfast Chana Masala   33

Leftover Curry with Fried Eggs   34

Indian-Style Savory "French" Toast   35

What's for breakfast? In India it could be anything; there aren't clear-cut distinctions on what constitutes a "breakfast" item as opposed to a "lunch" or "dinner" one. A lot of the things eaten in the morning could just as easily be served during other meals, or as a snack. Even eggs are eaten at any time of the day, not just for breakfast.

In this chapter, I've included some of the things I love making and eating in the morning. There's a wide variety, from eggs to flatbreads to curries. That's right, curry for breakfast; it's weird but wonderful. And as I've mentioned, none of these dishes have to strictly adhere to breakfast timings; you could as easily serve them at any other mealtime.

spicy coastal scramble

serves 4

If you like a scramble, you'll love my version. Redolent of curry leaves and coconut, it's an exotic twist on the familiar. And while it's fantastic at the breakfast table, like other Indian egg recipes it could just as naturally be served with steamed white rice for dinner.

10 fresh curry leaves, rinsed and patted dry
5 large eggs
2 tablespoons dried, shredded, unsweetened coconut
1 small green serrano chile, finely chopped

2 tablespoons minced shallot
¼ teaspoon Garlic Paste (page 14)
¼ teaspoon Ginger Paste (page 15)
Salt
3 tablespoons canola or coconut oil

Make a stack of the curry leaves, roll them over once, and slice them thickly. Crack the eggs into a large bowl and whisk with a fork. Add the curry leaves, coconut, green chile, shallot, garlic paste, ginger paste, and salt to the eggs and whisk together well.

Heat the oil in a heavy skillet set over high heat. Add the egg mixture to it and gently scramble. Don't let the eggs overcook and dry out—in fact, I like to cook this dish really soft, almost like a French omelet.

egg roll

makes 4 rolls

Despite the familiar name, this has absolutely nothing in common with Chinese take-out. My subcontinental egg roll is a thin omelet cooked in flatbread, then rolled up. Easy to carry, it's a perfect breakfast on the run.

4 large eggs
1 tablespoon minced red onion
1 tablespoon minced fresh cilantro
¼ teaspoon ground cumin

⅛ teaspoon ground turmeric
Salt
4 tablespoons canola oil
4 wheat tortillas

Break the eggs into a medium bowl. Add the onion, cilantro, cumin, turmeric, and salt and whisk well.

Heat a tablespoon of oil in a large nonstick skillet over medium heat. Pour a quarter of the whisked egg mixture into the skillet; it will spread out naturally. Place a tortilla on the omelet and let cook for a few moments—the omelet will adhere to the tortilla. Turn over and heat the tortilla side for a few seconds.

Transfer to a serving plate with the omelet side up and roll into a cylinder. Make the rest the same way.

eggless omelet

makes 6

While the name sounds like an oxymoron, eggless omelets are enjoyed by vegetarians all over western India for breakfast or as a snack. Similar to Italian *farinata*, these yummy savory pancakes are made of chickpea flour and are best eaten piping hot, straight off the skillet.

1½ cups *chana besan* (chickpea flour)
Salt
1¼ cups water
¼ cup minced red onion
¼ cup minced tomato

1 tablespoon minced fresh cilantro
¼ teaspoon Ginger Paste (page 15)
¼ teaspoon ground turmeric
1 small green serrano chile, minced
5 tablespoons canola oil

In a large mixing bowl, stir the *besan* and salt together, using a whisk. Gradually add the water. Whisk and break up all the little lumps to make a smooth batter of pouring consistency. Taste for, and adjust, the salt. Now stir in the onion, tomato, cilantro, ginger paste, turmeric, and chile.

Coat the bottom of an 8-inch nonstick skillet with a tablespoon of oil and heat over medium-high heat. Pour ¼ cup of the batter into the center of the pan and immediately swirl the pan to spread the batter into an 8-inch circle. Cook for 1 minute; it will have browned lightly on the underside. Flip it over, turn down the heat slightly, and cook on the other side until done—about 2 minutes.

Remove from the pan and serve, preferably right away. Refresh the skillet with a little more oil and continue as above until all the "omelets" are done.

gobi flatbread

makes 10

Packed with nutrition and taste, stuffed flatbreads are one of the few "dedicated" breakfast dishes in India, where they're made with all kinds of fillings: cauliflower, potatoes, even radish. My version uses *gobi* (cabbage). Serve with a bowl of Plain and Simple Raita (page 77) as a dip and Hot and Sweet Apple Chutney (page 152).

Dough
1½ cups whole wheat flour
½ cup all-purpose flour, plus extra
   for dusting
1 teaspoon kosher salt
2 tablespoons Ghee (page 13) or melted
   butter
1 cup warm water, or as needed, to make
   the dough

Filling
1 cup finely grated green cabbage
¼ teaspoon cumin seeds
1 medium serrano chile, seeded
   and minced
2 tablespoons finely chopped fresh cilantro
Salt

5 tablespoons canola oil, to roast the
   flatbread

Make the dough: You can either use a stand mixer or knead this dough by hand. If using a mixer, set it to low speed, using the dough hook attachment.

Stir the flours and salt together, add the ghee and rub it in well. Slowly add the water, mixing constantly until the dough comes together in a ball. Knead well until the dough is smooth and very pliant—about 7 minutes by hand, less if using a mixer. Set aside, covered with a damp cloth or plastic wrap, while you make the filling.

Make the filling: Using your fingers, squeeze out any moisture from the grated cabbage. Rub the cumin seeds between the palms of your dry hands (to release their essential oil) and add to the cabbage along with the chile, cilantro, and salt. Mix well and taste for salt.

Stuff the flatbread: Divide the dough into ten equal sections and roll each into a ball. Dust a work surface with some flour, and using a rolling pin, roll each ball into a 3-inch disk. Place a disk in the palm of your hand and spoon in a heaping tablespoon of the filling. Bring the edges of the dough over the filling and pinch together into a ball. Dust liberally with flour and roll gently into a 5- to 6-inch circle.

It takes a bit of practice to roll out a stuffed flatbread without breaking it, so initially it's okay to roll them slightly thicker. Flour the work surface and the bread as often as you need. Keep all dough covered with a clean, damp kitchen towel or it will dry out.

Roast the flatbread: Heat a dry heavy skillet on medium-high until very hot—a sprinkle of water should sizzle off right away. Place a stuffed flatbread on the hot skillet. When tiny bubbles appear on the surface of the flatbread—in about a minute—turn it over. Drizzle 1 teaspoon of the oil onto the skillet along the perimeter of the flatbread. After about a minute, it will lightly brown on the bottom. Use a pastry brush or the back of a spoon to smear ½ teaspoon of oil on the surface of the bread and turn it over.

Use a balled-up kitchen towel to press down the edges of the flatbread—these are the hardest areas to cook. The flatbread is done when it's golden brown on both sides and has no raw spots anywhere.

Roast the rest and place in a cloth-lined, covered container. Cover the container to keep the cooked flatbreads from drying out. Place a cloth napkin between the topmost flatbread and the container lid to keep the bread from sweating.

Tip

. . . .

Some markets carry "white" wheat flour that is closer to the soft wheat used in India. If you can find it, substitute it for both the flours in all bread recipes in this book.

indian grits with vegetables

serves 4

This mildly spiced, gritslike dish is a hit with both adults and kids. If your children have a problem with the "black seeds" (as my girls do), feel free to leave out the cumin and mustard.

4 tablespoons Ghee (page 13)
¼ teaspoon cumin seeds
¼ teaspoon mustard seeds
1 (½-inch) piece fresh ginger, minced
1 medium green serrano chile, chopped into ¼-inch rounds
1 shallot, finely chopped
5 cashews, coarsely chopped
¼ cup finely chopped carrots

¼ cup finely chopped green beans
¼ cup finely chopped cauliflower
¼ cup frozen peas, thawed, or fresh English peas, shelled
½ cup plain yogurt
1 cup hot water
Salt
1 cup coarse *rava* (farina/cream of wheat)

In a large wok or saucepan, heat the ghee over medium heat. When it just begins to smoke, add the cumin and mustard seeds and cover with a spatter screen or lid. When the sputtering stops, quickly add the ginger, chile, shallot, and cashews, and stir. After the shallot is lightly browned, add the carrots, green beans, cauliflower, and peas. Stir the vegetables until they are well coated with ghee and slightly softened.

Whisk the yogurt, water, and salt together and pour into the vegetables. Stir and bring to a boil over high heat. Turn down the heat and simmer, uncovered, until the vegetables are crisp-tender. Add the *rava,* stirring all the time. Cover tightly and steam until the *rava* is cooked and all the liquid is absorbed— 5 to 7 minutes.

kids' favorite banana fritters

makes 10

In Goa, these mini pancakes are called fritters. Guaranteed to please the fussiest kid, they're very much like banana pancakes, but heavier on the fruit, which makes them moister and richer tasting. I add a bit of *rava* to give the fritter a nicer texture, and a tiny amount of cardamom to uplift the batter without overpowering it. Keep away from adults, or the kids won't get any.

1 large egg
1 tablespoon granulated sugar
2 tablespoons milk
2 medium ripe bananas
¼ cup all-purpose flour
2 tablespoons *rava* (farina/cream of wheat)

⅛ teaspoon salt
1 whole green cardamom pod, peeled and
    finely ground to a powder
4 tablespoons unsalted butter

Whisk the egg, sugar, and milk together in a medium bowl. Add the bananas and mash with a fork, but keep the batter slightly lumpy. Mix well. Stir the flours, salt, and cardamom together and mix into the batter.

Heat a large nonstick skillet over medium heat. Add a tablespoon of butter and swirl the pan to melt it. Using a tablespoon measure, drop dollops of the batter into the skillet, smoothing with a spatula until each fritter is ¼ inch thick. Don't try to make them perfect rounds; odd shapes add to the charm of these delicious morsels. You can make up to four fritters at a time, depending on the size of your skillet.

Flip each fritter when you see tiny holes appear on the surface. It's ready when golden on both sides.

Serve hot with nothing but a napkin as an accompaniment.

comforting rice and yogurt

serves 4

This dish came about as a way to use up leftover rice. But it's so good, I make extra rice at dinner just so I can have this salad the next morning. Comforting, tasty, and nutritious, it's also perfect for young children, provided you take out the red chiles before serving. Tastes great cold or at room temperature.

4 cups precooked and cooled plain rice
2 cups plain yogurt, whisked lightly
Salt
2 tablespoons canola or peanut oil
¼ teaspoon mustard seeds

10 fresh curry leaves
2 dried red chiles, each broken in two
1 teaspoon *chana dal* (split chickpeas)
1 teaspoon unsalted toasted peanuts

Breaking up any lumps in the rice, mix it with the yogurt and add salt to taste. In a small skillet or butter warmer, heat the oil over high heat. When the oil just begins to smoke, add the mustard seeds and cover; they will pop loudly. As soon as the sputtering stops, add the curry leaves, dried chiles, *chana dal*, and finally, the peanuts. When the dal has browned, immediately take it off the heat and pour it over the rice mixture.

Tip

The crisp green leaves and toasty red chiles look beautiful sitting on top of the pristine white rice, so I don't mix in the dressing until I'm ready to actually eat it.

breakfast chana masala

serves 4

In the tiny coastal state of Goa, you can wander into any local café and order a plate of this piping hot chickpea curry for breakfast. Bursting with protein and dietary fiber, it starts your day right. Serve with a fresh bread roll, or if you want to indulge, a big Poofy Poori (page 122).

½ cup minced yellow onion
¼ cup dried, shredded,
    unsweetened coconut
1 tablespoon ground coriander
1 teaspoon ground cumin
½ teaspoon ground turmeric
1½ cups hot water

2 cups canned chickpeas, drained
1 medium green serrano chile,
    halved lengthwise
2 tablespoons minced fresh cilantro
1 tablespoon apple cider vinegar
Salt

In a heavy dry skillet, toast the onion and coconut over medium heat until browned. Transfer to a blender jar, add the coriander, cumin, turmeric, and ½ cup of the water, and blend until fine. Scrape out this mixture into a medium saucepan. Add the remaining 1 cup water to the blender and turn it on again, effectively washing it out. Pour this water into the saucepan, add the chickpeas and chile, and stir well. Place over high heat, and bring to a boil.

Turn down the heat to medium and cook for 12 minutes. Stir in the cilantro and vinegar and cook for a further 5 minutes. Taste and adjust with salt.

leftover curry with fried eggs

serves 4

In Goa, a traditional breakfast often includes *kaal chi kodi;* literally "yesterday's curry," cooked down to the consistency of a thick gravy. Since a coconut curry tastes even better the next day, the result is a dish everyone will be enthusiastically sopping up with crusty bread. I make it even better by serving it with eggs just laid by my neighbor's chickens.

1 cup Shortcut Shrimp-Okra Curry (page 134)
4 large eggs
Salt and freshly ground black pepper

Place the curry—shrimp, okra, and all—in a small pot and bring to a boil. Turn down the heat to a simmer and reduce the curry until there's only a ½-cup concentrate of thick, delicious, goodness left.

Fry the eggs as you normally would; I prefer mine cooked over high heat so the whites are browned and crisp while the yolks are still runny. Liberally sprinkle pepper all over, salt to taste, and serve alongside a few tablespoons of the rich, thickened curry.

Add a hunk of crusty bread and a cup of chai and you'll soon be transported to a breakfast table in Goa.

indian-style savory "french" toast

makes 8

Dip some day-old bread in a savory chickpea batter, pan-fry like French toast, and from humble beginnings, you'll end up with a rather fancy breakfast. Serve with Green Mint Relish (page 156) and good old tomato ketchup.

4 slices leftover sliced bread
½ cup *chana besan* (chickpea flour)
⅛ teaspoon cumin seeds
¼ teaspoon ground turmeric
¼ teaspoon cayenne

Salt
1 tablespoon minced fresh cilantro
¼ cup + 2 tablespoons water
½ cup canola oil, or as needed

Stack the bread and cut in half diagonally to make triangles. Place the *chana besan* in a mixing bowl large enough to accommodate the bread as well. Rub the cumin seeds between your palms (to release their essential oil) and add to the *chana besan*, along with the turmeric, cayenne, salt, and cilantro. Stir well and gradually mix in just enough water to achieve the consistency of a thin pancake batter.

Dip a single slice of bread in the batter, dunking it in to soak up some of the moisture and turning it so it's evenly coated.

Heat a medium nonstick skillet over high heat and pour 2 tablespoons of the oil into it. Turn down the heat to low and place the battered bread in the hot oil. It's okay to cook two slices at a time if they fit in the skillet comfortably. Don't overcrowd the pan or the oil will cool and the bread will end up absorbing most of it.

Cook the bread until golden brown on both sides, about 2 minutes per side. Remove from the pan and serve immediately. Repeat with the rest of the bread.

lightning lunches

Potato "Chops"   39

Grilled Chicken Wrap   40

Grilled Paneer and Beet Salad   41

Tata's Frankie Roll   42

Red Beef Sandwiches   44

Spicy Tuna Salad   45

Indian Veggie Burger   46

Corn Salad with Cracked Pepper   48

Chickpea Salad with Pomegranate   49

A Spicy Bowl of Peas   50

According to Ayurvedic principles, your digestive fire is strongest when the sun is highest in the sky and diminishes with the sun's progress down to the horizon. Consequently, you're supposed to eat an extremely light dinner, reserving the bulk of your appetite for lunch. That line of thinking is reflected in the afternoon *thali,* a huge affair with several vegetable dishes, dals, *raita,* and, depending on the region, a fish or meat curry, all served with lots of flatbread and rice.

Of course, the notion of pigging out at lunch followed by a refreshing siesta at your workplace, though tempting, is a bit impractical, to say the least. With that in mind, this chapter features several dishes I've created or adapted to fit a more modern lifestyle. When time is at a premium, you'll find these quick lunches are a snap to make, yet still very flavorful and nutritious.

potato "chops"

makes 6 chops

Frankly, I have no idea why they're called chops, but that's what you ask for when you're in Goa and you want the ultimate comfort food—crispy mashed potato on the outside, flavorful ground beef on the inside. They may also be the ultimate party food; you can form and refrigerate the chops up to a full day ahead and pan-fry when you're ready to serve them.

1 pound russet potatoes
½ cup + 2 tablespoons canola oil
½ medium yellow onion, minced
  (about 1 cup)
1 medium green serrano chile, seeded
  and minced
½ pound lean ground beef

½ teaspoon Green Masala (page 17)
Salt
⅛ teaspoon freshly ground black pepper
2 tablespoons minced fresh cilantro
1 large egg, whisked
½ cup *rava* (farina/cream of wheat) or fine
  bread crumbs

Scrub the potatoes and halve them. Boil in water in a covered pan until soft inside—about 8 minutes. Drain very well.

Meanwhile, in a large skillet, heat 2 tablespoons of the oil on high heat. Sauté the onion and chile together until the onion is soft and golden, about 3 minutes. Add the beef and cook, stirring constantly, breaking up any lumps. After the meat is all crumbly and cooked, add the green masala, salt to taste, pepper, and cilantro. Cook, stirring, for 3 to 4 minutes and remove from the heat.

While the beef is cooling, peel and mash the potatoes to a smooth consistency. You should get about 2 cups. Add salt to taste. Taking about 2 tablespoons of mashed potatoes

in your palm, flatten into a disk. Place a tablespoon of the beef mixture in the center and roll the mashed potatoes over it, forming a ball. Press into a 1½-inch-thick disk and place on a plate while you form the rest of the chops.

Place the whisked egg in a shallow bowl and the *rava* on a small plate. Dip each chop in the egg, then coat lightly with the *rava* and place on a clean plate.

After all the chops have been formed, heat the ½ cup of oil in a large pan over medium heat. When the oil starts rippling—about 375°F—gently place all the chops in the oil and pan-fry until golden on both sides, about 3 minutes per side.

grilled chicken wrap

makes 4 to 6 sandwiches

This is my Indianized take on a soft taco: spiced grilled chicken, wrapped in a pita bread and dressed up with a crunchy salad. With nearly every food group represented, you can fix a quick meal while packing in as much nutrition and taste as you can.

4 skinless, boneless chicken breasts (about 1½ pounds)
1 teaspoon Ginger Paste (page 15)
1 teaspoon Garlic Paste (page 14)
½ teaspoon ground turmeric
¼ teaspoon ground cumin
¼ teaspoon freshly ground black pepper
Salt
1 tablespoon apple cider vinegar
2 tablespoons canola oil
4 to 6 whole wheat pita breads
1 cup Indian Chopped Salad (page 70)

Rinse the chicken and pat dry. Mix the ginger paste, garlic paste, turmeric, cumin, pepper, salt to taste, and vinegar together to form a smooth paste and apply to the chicken, rubbing in well. Set aside in the refrigerator for 10 minutes, up to overnight.

Heat a cast-iron skillet over high heat and coat the bottom with the oil. Turn down the heat to medium and grill the chicken on both sides until cooked—no more than 10 minutes total. Set aside to cool slightly. Slice diagonally into large chunks.

Heat the pita bread slightly in a toaster oven, or in a microwave for a few seconds. Arrange the grilled chicken chunks down the center of each pita bread, top with a few tablespoons of the salad, and wrap loosely. Makes for a messy but yummy lunch.

Tip

For my kids, I smear a little "mayo-maize" (as my five-year-old calls it) on the pita bread first, making a moister and more kid-friendly wrap.

grilled paneer and beet salad

serves 4

Paneer is an Indian farmer cheese that behaves much like chèvre when grilled, forming a lovely golden crust outside while becoming meltingly tender inside. The grilled paneer pairs perfectly with arugula, and the beets make this salad hearty enough to be a main course.

2 large red beets
2 tablespoons freshly squeezed lemon juice
Salt and freshly ground black pepper
1 clove garlic, minced
1 tablespoon minced fresh cilantro
5 tablespoons canola oil

1 pound Paneer (page 20), cut into
 4 (2-inch) squares
¼ teaspoon ground turmeric
¼ teaspoon cayenne
¼ teaspoon ground cumin
3 cups tender arugula leaves, rinsed and dried

Boil the beets in water until cooked but still slightly firm inside (stick a paring knife into the center to check). Let cool, peel, and cut into ½-inch-thick half-moons.

In a small bowl, whisk the lemon juice, salt and pepper to taste, garlic, and cilantro together with 4 tablespoons of the oil to make a slightly tart dressing. Set aside.

Dust the paneer cubes with the turmeric, cayenne, cumin, and salt to taste. Heat a grill pan (preferably ridged) over high heat and brush with the remaining tablespoon of oil. Place the paneer squares in the pan and quickly grill them on both sides—about a minute per side.

Toss the beets and arugula with the dressing. Divide among four plates and top with the grilled paneer. Serve immediately.

tata's frankie roll

makes 6 to 8

This is my father's version of the famous Mumbai street food known as the Frankie (a regional variation of the also-famous Kathi roll). Frankies must be served hot off the skillet, so make sure you eat one right there in the kitchen, because the constant demands for "just one more" will keep you at the stove for quite a bit.

1 pound beef tenderloin, cut into
    ½-inch cubes
Salt
6½ tablespoons canola oil
2 cups thinly sliced yellow onion
½ teaspoon Ginger Paste (page 15)
½ teaspoon Garlic Paste (page 14)
¼ teaspoon ground turmeric
½ teaspoon cayenne

¼ teaspoon freshly ground black pepper
1 large tomato, minced (about ½ cup)
1 teaspoon Garam Masala (page 18)
4 eggs
2 tablespoons minced fresh cilantro
2 medium green serrano chiles, minced
1 lemon, quartered
6 to 8 (6-inch) whole wheat tortillas
    or chapatis

Sprinkle salt over the meat and set aside.

Heat 2½ tablespoons of the oil in a medium pan over high heat and sauté 1 cup of the onion until golden. Add the ginger paste, garlic paste, turmeric, cayenne, and pepper and cook, stirring, for another 3 to 4 minutes. Stir in the tomato and continue to cook over medium heat until the tomato has broken up and is pulpy. Add the meat and the garam masala and continue to cook, stirring constantly, until the beef is well coated with the sauce. Turn down the heat to low, cover, and cook until the beef is tender—about 10 minutes.

Whisk the eggs with a pinch of salt. In a small bowl, toss the remaining 1 cup of onion, the cilantro, and chiles with some salt and a squeeze of lemon. When ready to serve, place a stack of serving plates next to the stove.

Heat a large skillet on medium heat. Spread about 2 teaspoons of oil on the skillet. When the oil has heated, pour in 2 tablespoons of whisked egg; the egg will spread out naturally to form an omelet. Place a tortilla on the omelet and let cook for a few moments. Flip it out onto a serving plate, egg side up.

Place about 3 tablespoons of the curried beef down the length of one side of the tortilla. Sprinkle some of the onion salad on top, squeeze on some extra lemon juice, and then roll up the Frankie. If you like, wrap it in a napkin or secure it with a toothpick. Serve the first lucky eater and then continue making the rest.

Tip

. . . .

I use tenderloin because I like my meat soft; but if you prefer a slight chew to your beef, use top sirloin or another quick-cooking cut.

red beef sandwiches

serves 4

This is one of my quick-fix staples; I pack it for the kids' school lunch, serve it for a quick supper, or take it along for a picnic or road trip. It's incredibly simple to make and keeps really well. You can even cook the beef several hours ahead of time and store at room temp, stuffing it into the bread just before you dig in.

1 pound rib eye or top sirloin, sliced very
   thinly against the grain
Salt (approximately ¾ teaspoon kosher
   salt or to your liking)

2 tablespoons Red Masala (page 16)
4 tablespoons canola oil
4 mini French bread rolls

Rub the beef slices with salt and the red masala. Cover and set aside to marinate for 10 minutes or up to 2 days in the refrigerator.

Heat the oil in a large, heavy skillet over high heat and cook the beef slices—about 5 minutes. Be careful not to overcook the beef. And don't overcrowd the pan; cook in two batches if necessary.

Drain off any excess oil and distribute the red beef among the bread rolls. If the bread is good and fresh, you don't really need anything else. But if the sandwich is a bit too dry for you, smear a little aioli or mayonnaise on the bread and stuff in some red onion, tomato, and lettuce.

spicy tuna salad

makes a light lunch for 1

I first created this 5-minute salad to make use of leftover fish (obviously, I've never owned a cat). Then one day, with no leftovers on hand yet hankering for a nice spicy fish salad, I made it with a can of tuna and it turned out pretty good. This recipe makes a generous portion for one, so scale it up depending on how many last-minute folks you need to feed. Serve with water crackers or toast points.

1 (8-ounce) can water-packed tuna, drained, or 1 cup any leftover cooked fish
¼ cup minced red onion
¼ cup minced tomato
1 medium green serrano chile, seeded (if you prefer) and minced

2 tablespoons minced fresh cilantro
Lots of freshly ground black pepper
Pinch of cayenne
Small squeeze of lemon juice

Place the tuna in a large bowl, picking out any bones if you're using leftovers. Break it up with a fork and stir in the onion, tomato, chile, and cilantro. Stir well; sprinkle with the pepper, cayenne, and lemon juice; and toss again to mix.

Tip

You can make a lovely version of this salad with leftovers from the Baked Two-Pepper Sardines (page 89).

indian veggie burger

makes 4 patties

Having grown up in India, I've never really taken to veggie burgers in the West. Instead of soybeans or grains, a veggie burger in India is actually made of vegetables, bound with mashed potatoes and bread crumbs. Try my version and you'll never look at a store-bought veggie burger the same way again. The patty is delicious on its own with a little Green Mint Relish (page 46) and a green salad. Of course, you could also serve it in a bun with all the fixings.

½ pound medium russet potato (about 1 large), peeled, chopped into small pieces

2 ounces green beans (about 5), chopped into small pieces

2 ounces carrot (about 1 small), chopped into small pieces

4 ounces green cabbage (a small wedge), chopped into small pieces

¼ cup peas, fresh or frozen

2 ounces cauliflower (about 3 florets), chopped into small pieces

⅔ cup water

Salt

½ cup fresh bread crumbs, if needed

1 cup + 1 tablespoon canola or peanut oil

¼ cup minced shallot

1 small green serrano chile, minced

¼ teaspoon ground cumin

¼ teaspoon ground turmeric

¼ teaspoon cayenne (optional)

½ cup *rava* (farina/cream of wheat) or fine dry bread crumbs, for dusting

4 hamburger buns (optional)

Place the potato, green beans, carrot, cabbage, peas, and cauliflower in a large saucepan. Add the water and salt and bring to a boil. Reduce the heat, cover, and cook until the vegetables are completely soft—about 10 minutes. Let cool and mash well, but don't puree the mixture; a little lumpiness is fine. If it gets too loose, add some fresh bread crumbs.

In a small skillet, heat 1 tablespoon of oil over high heat and sauté the shallot and chile until well browned—about 3 minutes. Stir in the cumin, turmeric, and cayenne and sauté for another minute.

When cool, mix into the mashed vegetables and taste for seasoning; add a little more salt if necessary. Form into 3½-inch-wide and ½-inch-thick patties, coat with the dry *rava,* and set aside.

Heat the remaining 1 cup of oil in a large skillet until rippling. Lower in the patties and shallow-fry until browned on both sides— about 2 minutes per side.

Tip

Fresh bread crumbs help soak up excess
moisture in the vegetable mixture. To make
them, grind a couple of slices of fresh white
or wheat bread in a food processor. Dry bread
crumbs, on the other hand, are generally used
to coat something you're about to fry. You
can buy them, or just make your own by first
toasting some bread until crisp, then grinding
into a fine powder.

corn salad with cracked pepper

serves 4 as a snack, 2 as a light meal

Corn in India has always been a tough, starchy plant, defying a cook's best efforts to tame it. The most you could do was grill it over open coals, then rub it down with lemon and salt, as the street food vendors did. Those limitations vanished when we finally got American corn. The first time I saw it in Mumbai, the vendor had a huge sign on his cart that said, "Bush's Corn." Whatever your politics, I think you'll like the savory corn salad I created that day.

4 medium Yukon Gold potatoes
2 ears white corn, husked
2 ears yellow corn, husked
1 tablespoon canola or peanut oil
1 small yellow onion, minced (about 1 cup)
1 clove garlic, minced

20 curry leaves, chiffonaded finely
 (see tip)
Salt
1 tablespoon minced fresh cilantro
Whole black peppercorns

Boil the potatoes until tender, then let cool and cut each potato into ½-inch cubes. Using a sharp knife, cut the kernels off each ear of corn.

Heat the oil in a wok over high heat and sauté the onion and garlic in it until the onion is browned. Add the corn kernels, potatoes, curry leaves, and salt to taste, and toss.

Turn down the heat to medium-low, cover, and cook until the corn is tender—about 5 minutes. Stir in the cilantro and coarsely grind some pepper over.

Serve warm or at room temperature.

Tip

. . . .

To chiffonade means "to cut into ribbons." Stack all the curry leaves one on top of the other, roll into a tiny cigar shape, and then slice crosswise into thin strips.

chickpea salad with pomegranate

serves 6 to 8

This recipe is loosely based on potato *chaat,* a popular street food that's deliciously spicy and tangy. My version has all of that flavor, but it's also a treat for the eyes, with the red and purple potatoes and jewel-like pomegranate seeds standing out against the green of the herbs.

1¼ pounds red, purple, and/or
    fingerling potatoes
1 (14-ounce) can chickpeas, drained
    and rinsed
1 teaspoon ground cumin
¼ teaspoon cayenne
¼ teaspoon ground ginger
¼ teaspoon freshly ground black pepper
5 tablespoons freshly squeezed lemon juice,
    or to taste

5 tablespoons canola or peanut oil
Salt
½ cup fresh pomegranate seeds
2 tablespoons minced fresh mint, plus a
    few whole leaves for garnish
2 tablespoons minced fresh cilantro
1 large, ripe tomato, halved and thinly sliced
1 small red onion, halved and thinly sliced
1 small green serrano chile, minced

Place the potatoes in a medium saucepan, cover with water, and bring to a boil. Cook until tender but still firm. Let cool and cut into ½-inch cubes.

Place the chickpeas and potatoes in a large bowl. Add the cumin, cayenne, ginger, black pepper, lemon juice, and oil to the potato mixture and toss well. Taste and, if needed, add a little salt. Add the pomegranate seeds, mint, cilantro, tomato, onion, and chile and toss again gently. Garnish with the whole mint leaves.

Serve cold or at room temperature.

a spicy bowl of peas

serves 4

A bowlful of peas for lunch may sound unusual. But this dish doesn't do too well in a secondary role, preferring to star on its own as a hearty lunch accompanied by a nice crusty loaf of bread. It's best made at the height of summer, when there's an abundance of fresh English peas. Of course, you could make it any time of year with frozen peas, but avoid petite peas as they're a bit too sweet for the recipe.

2 tablespoons canola or untoasted
   sesame oil
¼ teaspoon mustard seeds
¼ teaspoon ground turmeric
½ teaspoon cayenne

1 pound peas, fresh or frozen
Salt (approximately ½ teaspoon kosher
   salt or to your liking)
1½ cups water
2 tablespoons minced fresh cilantro

Heat the oil in a medium saucepan over high heat. When the oil just begins to smoke, add the mustard seeds. When they've stopped sputtering, add the turmeric, cayenne, and peas. Stir well, add salt and the water, and bring to a boil. Turn down the heat, cover, and simmer until the peas are cooked—between 5 and 10 minutes, depending on how tender the peas were.

Stir in the cilantro, ladle into bowls, and serve hot. Serve with French bread, flatbread, or even plain steamed rice. I happily eat bowl after bowl just by itself.

swift
soups

Tomato Water   55

Incendiary Pepper Water   56

Wholesome Spinach Dal Soup   57

Chicken and Cilantro-Lime Soup   58

Cold Buttermilk Soup   60

Minestrone for Mira   61

Hearty Beef Soup with Turmeric   62

The "soup course" hasn't traditionally been a part of Indian cuisine. There are exceptions, of course. That old Anglo-Indian favorite Mulligatawny comes to mind. And there's the state of Goa, which was ruled by the Portuguese for centuries, making *sopa* part of the local diet. My Hearty Beef Soup with Turmeric hails from there.

As for the rest of India, there are all kinds of soupy dishes served during the meal that, from a Western perspective, would make a fine first course. These include Tomato Water and Incendiary Pepper Water. Then there are other preparations that are normally served over rice, such as my Wholesome Spinach-Dal Soup—you'll find it does very well on its own. The same goes for Cold Buttermilk Soup.

This section also includes some of my own recipes, such as Chicken and Cilantro Soup and Minestrone for Mira. These came about because my children love soup and I wanted to add a few with distinctly Indian flavors to our family table.

tomato water

serves 4

Tomato Water evolved out of frugality, a clever way to extend a limited amount of dal. Cooked dal eventually settles to the bottom of the pot, leaving a layer of thin liquid floating on top. Instead of discarding this flavorful stock, Maharashtrian cooks decant it, turning it into an entirely new and delicious preparation. I make Tomato Water as a dish in its own right, starting only with a few tablespoons of dal.

3 tablespoons *masoor dal* (split pink lentils)
2 cups minced tomatoes
1 Indian bay leaf
8 whole peppercorns
1 (1-inch) stick cinnamon
5 cups water

½ teaspoon granulated sugar
Salt
½ teaspoon cayenne
2 tablespoons Ghee (page 13)
1 teaspoon cumin seeds
10 fresh curry leaves (optional)

Place the dal, tomatoes, bay leaf, peppercorns, cinnamon stick, and 4 cups of the water in a large pan and bring to a boil. Cook on medium-high heat until the dal is tender—about 20 minutes. Let cool slightly, pick out and discard the bay leaf and cinnamon stick, then transfer to a blender and puree. Strain the soup back into the pan. Add the additional 1 cup water, the sugar, salt to taste, and cayenne and bring back to a boil.

Heat the ghee in a small skillet or butter warmer over high heat. When the ghee just begins to smoke, add the cumin seeds and cover. When the sputtering stops, add the curry leaves, if using. Once the leaves have finished sizzling, pour the hot dressing over the tomato water.

incendiary pepper water

serves 4 to 6

The name isn't an overstatement. Served scalding hot, this spicy, tangy South Indian concoction hits you in the back of the throat. Once the shock wears off, it begins warming you up, chasing away your rainy-day blues. With a very different kind of heat than red chiles, pepper water is used to aid digestion, clear the sinuses, and soothe a fever. On the other hand, my husband, an amateur mixologist, serves ice-cold shots of it (minus the carrots), spiked with vodka.

1 teaspoon ground cumin
1 teaspoon freshly ground black pepper
2 large cloves garlic, peeled
35 fresh curry leaves, rinsed
2 cups finely chopped tomatoes

4 cups water
Salt
4 baby carrots, thinly sliced into rounds
2 tablespoons freshly squeezed lime juice

Combine the cumin, pepper, garlic, curry leaves, and tomatoes in a blender jar and puree until absolutely fine.

Pour into a large saucepan, add the water and bring to a boil. Salt to taste and cook at a low boil for 5 minutes. Add the sliced carrots. Continue to simmer for another 5 minutes, or until the carrots are crisp-tender. Stir in the lemon juice and serve piping hot!

Tip

This soup tends to separate when it sits, so remember to stir before serving. I like the resulting cloudy appearance and the occasional taste of a gritty spice; it adds to the overall heady experience. But you may also strain the soup if you prefer. Do this before you add the carrots, then continue with the rest of the recipe.

wholesome spinach-dal soup

serves 4

Dal, the soupy preparation made from dried lentils or beans, is the foundation of Indian cooking, the one protein eaten in every corner of the subcontinent, whether you're a vegetarian or not. This recipe adds spinach for twice the flavor and goodness. It makes a delicious soup, but you can also enjoy it over rice, as part of a larger Indian menu. Or just add a piece of crusty bread and call it supper.

¾ cup *chana dal* (split chickpeas)
4 cups water
2 tablespoons canola oil
⅓ cup minced yellow onion
2 whole cloves
¼ teaspoon ground turmeric

1 teaspoon ground coriander
1 cup finely shredded spinach
Salt
1 tablespoon Ghee (page 13)
½ teaspoon cumin seeds
3 large cloves garlic, minced

Rinse and soak the *chana dal* in hot water to cover for at least 10 minutes or up to 4 hours.

Drain, top with 3 cups of fresh water, and bring to a boil. Turn down the heat to medium, cover, and cook until the dal is soft but still retains its shape—about 20 minutes.

While the dal is cooking, heat the oil in a medium saucepan. Sauté the onion and whole cloves until the onion is well browned. Stir in the turmeric and coriander, then add the spinach and cook until soft.

When the dal has softened, pour it into the spinach, add the remaining cup of water and salt to taste, and bring to a boil. Turn down the heat and simmer for 4 minutes.

Heat the ghee in a small skillet over medium-high heat. When the ghee just begins to smoke, add the cumin seeds and cover. When the sputtering stops, add the garlic and cook until well browned. Pour over the soup and serve hot.

chicken and cilantro-lime soup

serves 4

For such a simple recipe, this clear soup is very refined and I often serve it when we have company. If you prefer your soup heartier, just add some poached chicken.

1½ tablespoons canola oil
¼ cup minced yellow onion
1 teaspoon minced garlic
⅛ teaspoon freshly ground black pepper
¼ teaspoon ground turmeric
½ teaspoon ground cumin
½ teaspoon ground coriander
½ cup peeled, chopped, canned tomatoes

5 cups homemade or canned
    chicken stock
Salt
1 small handful of tender cilantro stalks
    with leaves, hand torn roughly
2½ tablespoons freshly squeezed lime
    juice, or more to taste

Heat the oil over medium heat in a stockpot. Sauté the onion and garlic for 2 minutes, or until softened. Stir in the black pepper, turmeric, cumin, and coriander and sauté for an additional minute. Add the tomatoes, cover, and cook until the tomatoes break down—3 to 4 minutes. Using a wooden spatula, mash the tomatoes until pulpy. Add the chicken stock to the pot. Add salt to taste and bring to a boil. Turn down the heat and simmer for 5 minutes so that all the flavors blend together well.

Stir in the cilantro and lime juice and serve piping hot.

Tip

Be sure to add the cilantro leaves at the very last minute before serving, as the herb doesn't reheat too well.

cold buttermilk soup

serves 4

The name may sound unusual, but I think you'll become a fan once you've tasted the garlicky goodness of this cold soup. I often serve it with a really spicy meal like Singapore-style crab; it helps tame the heat of the main dish and becomes an elegant counterpoint to the crab-cracking frenzy.

¼ teaspoon cumin seeds
2 large cloves garlic
4 cups low-fat buttermilk

1 (14-ounce) can coconut milk, shaken well
Salt

Toast the cumin seeds in a dry skillet until lightly browned and fragrant. Let cool and grind finely to a powder (see Tip). Peel and lightly crush the garlic, but take care to leave the cloves whole—they'll be easier to pick out later.

Combine the cumin, garlic, buttermilk, coconut milk, and salt to taste in a glass bowl and stir well. Let the soup sit in the refrigerator for 10 minutes for all the flavors to meld.

Tip

Grinding such a small quantity of cumin seeds in a spice grinder is a bit of a challenge, so use a mortar and pestle instead. And if the possibility of biting down on raw garlic scares you, fish it out before serving.

minestrone for mira

serves 4

When my daughter first began to eat solids, I was always devising ways of getting as many veggies into her as possible. This one was a winner in my book, and apparently in Mira's as well; she's now eight years old and I'm still making this soup for her, and for her little sister, too. There are no hard-and-fast rules in this recipe; you can vary the vegetables to your taste or that of your child.

2 tablespoons unsalted butter
½ cup finely chopped red onion
1 small Indian bay leaf
2 large cloves garlic, minced
¼ teaspoon ground turmeric
2 cups chopped mixed vegetables (¼-inch cubes) (I like a mix of broccoli, yellow zucchini, carrots, green beans, spinach, cabbage, and green peas)

1 small Yukon Gold potato, cut into ¼-inch cubes
2 tablespoons *masoor dal* (split pink lentils)
¼ teaspoon dried oregano
2 cups chopped tomatoes
3 cups water or chicken stock
Salt (approximately ¾ teaspoon kosher salt or to your liking)
½ cup cooked macaroni (optional)

Place the butter in a stockpot over high heat and sauté the onion, bay leaf, garlic, and turmeric for 1 minute. Add the mixed vegetables, potato, dal, and oregano and sauté for an additional minute. Stir in the tomatoes and sauté until pulpy—about 3 minutes.

Add the water and salt and bring to a boil. Turn down the heat and simmer until the vegetables are cooked—20 to 25 minutes.

Add the cooked macaroni, if using, to the soup, stir, and serve warm.

Tip

Oregano in Indian cooking? I've used it here to emulate the Indian spice *ajwain* that I'd normally use. *Ajwain* tastes quite like oregano and shares its excellent digestive properties.

hearty beef soup with turmeric

serves 4

This soup is based on a beef broth from Goa. In the traditional recipe, a beef shank is simmered for hours with a piece of dried turmeric root. I took it a bit further, adding a few more spices and some rice; now everyone in my extended family makes it this way. A meal in itself, it's an excellent soup for kids. If you like, you can add some finely chopped carrots and dispense with the vegetable course completely.

1 tablespoon canola oil
1 cup minced yellow onion
6 large cloves garlic, peeled and smashed
1 Indian bay leaf
½ teaspoon ground turmeric
4 ounces beef top sirloin, cut into
   ¼-inch pieces

¼ teaspoon freshly ground black pepper
½ teaspoon ground coriander
¼ cup minced tomato
5 cups beef stock or broth
½ cup uncooked short-grain rice
Salt

Heat the oil in a large stockpot and sauté the onion, garlic, and bay leaf over high heat for 1 minute, stirring constantly. Add the turmeric and beef and cook, stirring, until the beef has browned well. Stir in the pepper, coriander, and tomato and sauté for an additional 2 minutes.

Pour in the stock and bring to a boil. Add the rice and a little salt if needed, turn down the heat, and simmer for 20 minutes, or until the rice is soft and the beef is cooked.

speedy salads and raitas

Sprouted Mung Bean Salad   67

Tomato and Onion Koshimbeer   68

Shredded Carrot Coconut Salad   68

Indian Chopped Salad   70

Pickled Cucumber and Carrot Salad   71

Banana Raita with Cayenne   72

Beet Raita with Cilantro   72

Cucumber Raita with Curry Leaves   74

Potato Raita with Cumin   75

Butternut Squash Raita with Peanuts   76

Plain and Simple Raita   77

Until fairly recently, salad greens weren't widely cultivated in India. There was no need; all leafy greens were the kind that went into the cooking pot. So when McDonald's came to India, it had to bring everything to its new location—from the seeds to the refrigerated transportation system—just to grow iceberg lettuce.

For most Indians, a salad is neither leafy nor a stand-alone dish. And it's meant to be eaten in small quantities alongside the rest of your meal. This may sound baffling if your whole idea of salad is a huge bowl of leafy greens, but run with it. Just remember that when the recipe says it serves four, it means four people eating a couple of tablespoons each.

A *raita* is a yogurt-based salad; it provides a cooling complement to an otherwise rich meal. You could make it with a vegetable, a fruit, or even with plain yogurt if you're in a hurry. Salads and *raitas* may be dressed simply with lemon juice or vinegar, but a hot oil dressing may also be added for a burst of flavor.

sprouted mung bean salad

serves 4

At the sprouting stage, mung beans are simply bursting with nutrition; they're also a lot easier to digest. I serve sprouts every day, and this simple, tasty recipe is the one I use most often. By the way, I always grow my own sprouts; it's easy and avoids any possibility of contamination. If you'd like to do the same, follow the directions at the end of this recipe.

2 cups mung bean sprouts
¼ cup minced red onion
1 tablespoon minced fresh cilantro
1 small green serrano chile, minced
Salt

½ teaspoon granulated sugar
Juice of ½ lemon, or as needed
1 tablespoon canola or peanut oil
½ teaspoon mustard seeds

In a serving bowl, lightly mix the sprouted beans with the onion, cilantro, chile, salt, sugar, and lemon juice. Taste and adjust the salt, lemon juice, and sugar—the salad should taste slightly tangy.

Heat the oil in a small skillet or butter warmer over high heat. When the oil just begins to smoke, add the mustard seeds and cover. The seeds will pop loudly. When the popping stops, immediately take off the heat and pour the hot oil dressing over the salad and mix.

Serve cold or at room temperature.

Tip

If you don't like raw sprouts, lightly steam them: Bring a pan of salted water to a rolling boil. Put the sprouts in a colander or strainer and place over the boiling water, cover, and steam for no more than 2 to 3 minutes. Remove from the steamer, let cool, and proceed with the recipe.

To sprout your own beans

Rinse 1 cup of mung beans and soak them overnight with plenty of water to cover. The next morning, drain the beans and place in a clear glass bowl. Cover with cheesecloth and keep in a warm place until they sprout; this could take several days in cold weather. Once a day, rinse them in fresh water and return to the covered bowl—this keeps them from getting moldy. Be patient and very soon you'll be rewarded with little shoots. I always have a batch at some stage of germination, so as to have a daily supply of sprouts. Finally, remember that you can sprout many kinds of beans, not just mung.

Serves 4

tomato-onion koshimbeer

serves 4

Combining tomatoes, onion, and cilantro, this easy salad may resemble pico de gallo, but it's a regular fixture on most Maharashtrian tables. The hot oil dressing adds a smoky flavor and that's where the recipe moves away from its Mexican counterpart.

1 cup minced ripe tomatoes
½ cup minced red onion
1 small green serrano chile, minced
1 tablespoon minced fresh cilantro
Salt
1 tablespoon canola or peanut oil
¼ teaspoon mustard seeds

Mix the tomatoes, onion, chile, cilantro, and salt to taste in a serving bowl.

Heat the oil in a small skillet or butter warmer over high heat. When the oil just begins to smoke, add the mustard seeds and cover. The seeds will pop loudly. When the popping stops, immediately take off the heat and pour the hot oil dressing into the salad. Mix well and serve.

shredded carrot coconut salad

serves 4

Adding a little coconut gives this salad a fresh, exotic flavor.

8 ounces medium carrots, shredded
   (use a box grater)
3 tablespoons shredded, dried,
   unsweetened coconut
1 small green serrano chile, minced
1 tablespoon minced fresh cilantro
1 tablespoon freshly squeezed lime juice
Salt
1 tablespoon canola or peanut oil
¼ teaspoon mustard seeds

Mix the shredded carrots in a serving bowl with the coconut, chile, cilantro, lime juice, and salt to taste.

Heat the oil in a small skillet or butter warmer over high heat. When the oil just begins to smoke, add the mustard seeds and cover. When the popping stops, immediately take off the heat and pour the hot oil dressing into the shredded carrots. Mix well and serve.

indian chopped salad

serves 4 to 6

This salad defies all vegetable-slicing logic; any trained chef would wince at the different sizes of each ingredient in this dish. But what can I say; it works very well and it's a favorite in my house. The kids love to make it and eat it, and it's an easy way to get several vegetables into them at one shot.

1 medium red beet
¼ wedge small green cabbage
1 medium carrot, peeled
1 medium cucumber, peeled
1 medium juice orange
1 small shallot, minced
1 small tomato, minced

2 tablespoons minced fresh cilantro
2 medium green serrano chiles, seeded
   and minced
2 tablespoons freshly squeezed lemon
   juice, or more to taste
Salt

Boil the beet in water to cover. Cook until the tip of a paring knife slides easily into the outside inch of the beet—the core should still be crisp. This should take about 8 minutes. Let cool, peel, and slice thinly into half-moon shapes.

Using a sharp knife, shred the cabbage thinly into inch-long pieces. Place the shredded cabbage in ice water—this makes it crisp.

Shred the carrot on the medium side of a grater. Slice the cucumber into quarters lengthwise and then crosswise into thin triangles.

Segment the orange and cut away any pith. The best way to do this is to first peel the fruit, using a sharp paring knife, and then cut out the segments from within their fibrous homes.

Mix everything together in a serving bowl and adjust the salt and lemon juice. This tangy salad is best served cold, so refrigerate until ready to serve.

pickled cucumber and carrot salad

serves 4

In this recipe, the cucumbers and carrots are sliced so thin that the lemon juice instantly pickles them. This tangy salad also works as an appetizer—give everyone a tiny fork to use to fish out a thin sliver of carrot or cucumber.

2 medium cucumbers, preferably
  English, peeled
2 medium carrots, peeled
2 medium green serrano chiles, seeded
1 tablespoon minced fresh cilantro

3 tablespoons freshly squeezed lemon
  juice, or to taste
Salt
¼ teaspoon granulated sugar

Using a mandoline or the slicer side of a box grater, slice the cucumbers and carrots into very thin rounds. Using a knife, cut the chiles into thin rounds as well.

In a serving bowl, mix together the cucumbers, carrots, chiles, cilantro, lemon juice, salt to taste, and sugar. Use your fingers; this distributes the dressing evenly, otherwise the slices of cucumber tend to stick together in a clump. Let sit in the refrigerator for at least 10 minutes before serving.

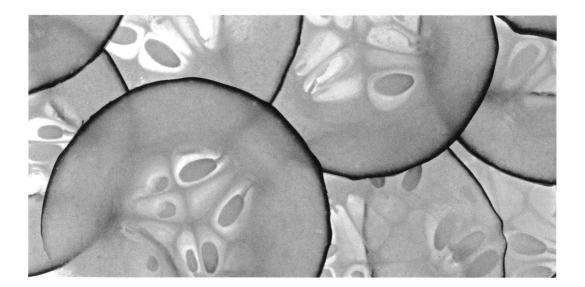

banana raita with cayenne

serves 4

Here's an example of a fruit *raita* that's simple to make, yet complex in taste. The sweetness of the bananas contrasts really nicely with the mildly spiced yogurt in this unusual *raita.*

1 cup plain yogurt
Salt
Pinch of granulated sugar
¼ teaspoon cayenne
2 ripe but firm bananas, cut into
   ½-inch-thick slices

Stir the yogurt, salt, sugar, and cayenne together in a serving bowl. Add the sliced bananas to the yogurt. That's it!

beet raita with cilantro

serves 4

I love beets, and I especially love them in this head-turning dish. When you add the beets, the yogurt turns a lovely pink. Just be sure to add the beets right before service or you'll get too much of a good thing; the longer they sit in the yogurt, the deeper the color. And despite what my younger daughter, Lola, says, purple is not better than pink.

1 medium beet
1 cup plain yogurt
¼ teaspoon ground cumin
1 tablespoon minced red onion
1 tablespoon minced fresh cilantro
1 tablespoon freshly squeezed lime juice
½ teaspoon granulated sugar

Boil the beet until soft—about 10 minutes. Let cool, peel, and cut into ½-inch pieces; you need about 1 cup for this recipe. In a serving bowl, mix the yogurt, cumin, onion, cilantro, lime juice, and sugar. Stir in the beets when you're ready to serve.

cucumber raita with curry leaves

serves 4

With influences from various regions of India, my version of cucumber *raita* is a bit different than the usual. I dress it with hot mustard oil that's been infused with curry leaves and serrano chile. The result is a very sophisticated, complex *raita*.

1 English or other cucumber
½ teaspoon mustard seeds
1 cup plain yogurt, whisked
Salt
¼ teaspoon ground turmeric

1 tablespoon canola or untoasted
    sesame oil
10 fresh curry leaves
1 small green serrano chile, cut into
    thin rounds

If the cucumber is too waxy, peel it first. Otherwise rinse well and grate on the large holes of a grater.

Crush half the mustard seeds to a powder, using the back of a spoon or your mortar and pestle.

In a serving bowl, stir together the yogurt, salt, cucumber, and crushed mustard. Place the turmeric in a little pile on the surface of the yogurt—do not mix in.

In a small skillet or butter warmer, heat the oil over high heat. When it just begins to smoke, add the remaining mustard seeds and cover. After they've stopped popping, promptly add the curry leaves and chile to the hot oil and step back—it'll be quite a wild dance in the pan. The curry leaves and chile will turn crisp within seconds. Immediately remove from the heat and pour the hot oil dressing over the turmeric pile.

Tip

The crisp leaves and turmeric oil look gorgeous against the white yogurt, so don't stir the dressing into the *raita* until your guests have had a chance to see your creation. By the way, a slightly tart yogurt works better for this *raita,* so choose your brand accordingly.

potato raita with cumin

serves 4

Here's a lovely way to present your potato salad for Thanksgiving. Toasted cumin seeds add an exotic Indian flavor, while the smooth yogurt contrasts with the starchiness of the potato to create a very comforting dish.

1 medium russet potato
1 cup plain yogurt
Salt
Pinch of granulated sugar

1 tablespoon canola or untoasted
    sesame oil
¼ teaspoon cumin seeds
¼ teaspoon cayenne

Boil the potato until nice and tender but not falling apart. Let cool, peel, and cut into 1-inch cubes. Meanwhile, stir the yogurt, salt, and sugar together in a serving bowl. When the potato cubes are completely cool, stir into the yogurt and adjust the salt to taste.

Heat the oil in a small skillet or butter warmer over high heat. When the oil just begins to smoke, add the cumin seeds and cover. When the sputtering stops, immediately take off the heat, stir in the cayenne, and pour the hot oil dressing over the *raita*.

Tip

A hot oil dressing must be made right before using; the dressing needs to be hot to transfer its smoky flavor to the dish.

butternut squash raita with peanuts

serves 4

My home state of Maharashtra is famous for the multitude of interesting ways that vegetables are prepared—even hard-core vegetarians from other states tend to be impressed by these permutations and combinations. When I was growing up, there'd usually be at least three different vegetable dishes on my plate. Here's a typical example: Squash is steamed and then dressed with crushed peanuts and yogurt. Butternut works great, but you could also use pumpkin or any other orange-fleshed hard squash.

1 pound butternut squash, peeled and cut into 1-inch cubes
½ cup water
1 cup plain yogurt, whisked
2 tablespoons fresh cilantro, finely chopped
⅓ cup ground peanuts (raw or toasted)

Pinch of granulated sugar
Salt
1 tablespoon Ghee (page 13)
¼ teaspoon cumin seeds
1 fresh serrano chile, chopped finely

Place the cubed squash in a medium pan with the water, cover, and steam until soft—about 7 minutes. Lightly mash the squash (a lumpy texture is desirable) with a fork and let cool.

Stir the yogurt with the cilantro, peanuts, sugar, and salt in a serving bowl. Gently mix the squash into the yogurt.

Heat the ghee in a small skillet or butter warmer over high heat. When the ghee just begins to smoke, add the cumin seeds and cover. When the sputtering stops, add the green chile. When the chile is toasted, pour the hot dressing over the *raita*. Stir and serve.

plain and simple raita

makes 1 cup

It doesn't get any simpler than this. Just spike some yogurt with a little cumin and pepper and you've got a highly versatile *raita.* Use it to tame a spicy curry, as a dip for kebabs, or just drizzle it over fresh fruit.

1 cup plain whole or low-fat yogurt (in my opinion, nonfat has zero flavor)
Salt
¼ teaspoon ground cumin

Pinch of freshly ground black pepper
Pinch of granulated sugar if the yogurt is particularly tart

Using a small whisk or fork, stir together the yogurt, salt, cumin, pepper, and sugar, if using, in a serving bowl until the *raita* has a pouring consistency. If it's still too thick for your liking, thin it out with 1 or 2 tablespoons of water. This *raita* will keep in the refrigerator for up to 2 days.

mains in minutes

Red Braised Chicken   81

Green Pan-Roasted Chicken   82

Lamb Seekh Kebabs   83

Stir-fried Beef with Peppers   84

Spicy Shell-on Red Shrimp   86

Black Pepper Shrimp with Curry Leaves   87

Coriander Shrimp with Zucchini   88

Baked Two-Pepper Sardines   89

Braised Halibut with Green Masala   90

Pan-Fried Silky Eggplant   91

Garlicky Pattypan Squash   92

Mushroom Chile Fry   94

Gingery Paneer with Red Peppers   95

Baby Potatoes in Green Masala Sauce   96

A typical Indian meal consists of several dishes of relatively equal importance, all eaten together. So if you're more accustomed to mains and sides, how do you plan a menu? That's where this section comes in; it gives you a main protein to build the rest of the meal around.

To help you along, I've provided serving suggestions with every recipe here. You can choose one side dish from the list for an everyday meal or all of them for a more elaborate affair. Then again, you can ignore the suggestions completely, fitting the dishes from this section into your regular menus. For example, I often serve my Red Braised Chicken with a ratatouille and a green salad. It may not be traditional, but it tastes great.

I've also included five vegetable dishes that are hearty enough to be the main attraction. If you're not a vegetarian, it may seem strange to build a meal around a sautéed vegetable. But follow the serving suggestions and you'll end up with a balanced, tasteful, and exotic vegetarian meal.

red braised chicken

serves 4

While it's not essential to marinate the chicken in this recipe, it really does "kick it up a notch," to borrow a phrase. I'd let it keep for at least the 10 minutes mentioned here. If you have the time, marinate for longer; you'll actually be making the recipe quicker by breaking it up into two parts. Let's say you rub the red masala into the chicken before leaving for work in the morning. When you get home, just put the chicken on to braise while you sip a glass of wine. Twenty minutes later, you'll be sitting down to a succulent braised chicken for dinner.

1 (3½-pound) chicken, skinned and cut
    into 8 pieces
4 tablespoons Red Masala (page 16)
2 tablespoons apple cider vinegar

1 teaspoon granulated sugar
Salt
4 tablespoons canola oil

Rinse and pat dry the chicken. In a small bowl, stir together the red masala, vinegar, sugar, and salt. Taste the mixture—it should taste spicy and tangy with a good balance between sweet and sour. Adjust accordingly, adding more vinegar, sugar, or salt. Apply this mixture to the chicken, rubbing it in well. Cover and leave to marinate for 10 minutes on the counter, or up to overnight in the refrigerator.

Heat the oil in a large pan over medium heat and add the chicken, making sure not to overcrowd the pan. Brown the chicken well on all sides, turning occasionally. Turn down the heat to low, cover, and cook until the chicken is done—about 20 minutes.

Serving suggestion: Wok-Fried Potatoes (page 104), Beet Raita with Cilantro (page 72), Shredded Carrot Coconut Salad (page 68).

green pan-roasted chicken

serves 4 to 6

Here's another easy recipe with huge depth of flavor. The secret is adding whole spices to the hot oil before you toss in the chicken. And remember, this is supposed to be a "dry" roasted dish; once it's done, there should be just a bit of thick sauce, if any. So if the chicken has given off too much moisture, continue to heat the pan over high heat until only a lovely glaze remains.

3 pounds chicken parts, skinned
Salt
3 tablespoons Green Masala (page 17)
4 tablespoons canola oil

1 teaspoon black peppercorns
1 (3-inch) stick cinnamon
6 whole cloves
2 medium carrots, cut into 1-inch pieces

Rinse and pat dry the chicken, then salt generously. Add the green masala, rubbing it in well. Cover and leave to marinate for 10 minutes on the counter, or up to overnight in the refrigerator.

Heat the oil in a large pan over medium heat and add the peppercorns, cinnamon stick, and cloves. After the spices are toasted—about 10 seconds—add the chicken to the hot

oil, making sure not to overcrowd the pan. Brown the chicken well on all sides, turning occasionally. Add the carrots and toss again. Turn down the heat to low, cover, and cook until the chicken is done—about 20 minutes.

Serving suggestion: Butternut Squash Raita with Peanuts (page 76), Mustardy Mashed Potatoes (page 106), and some crusty bread.

lamb seekh kebabs

makes 12 kebabs

Yes, you can make this restaurant staple at home. What's more, seekh kebabs are really quick to make. It takes a bit of practice to form them on a skewer; keep a bowl of water handy and wet your palms frequently as you work. And if it seems too daunting, forget the skewers and just hand form the mixture into 4-inch-long cylindrical shapes.

2 pounds ground lamb (not too lean)
1 teaspoon ground cumin
½ teaspoon ground coriander
½ teaspoon cayenne
¼ cup minced yellow onion
¼ cup minced fresh ginger
¼ cup minced fresh cilantro

1 medium green serrano chile, minced
2 eggs, whisked
Salt
¼ cup melted Ghee (page 13), for basting
Lemon wedges and thinly sliced red onion, for serving

Combine the ground lamb with the cumin, coriander, cayenne, onion, ginger, cilantro, chile, eggs, and salt. Knead well, using your fingers. Let the mixture rest for about 15 minutes.

Form the seekh kebabs: Divide the lamb mixture into twelve equal balls. Wet your palms and press a lamb ball along the length of a skewer, making a 4-inch-long kebab. Repeat with the rest of the lamb mixture and skewers.

You can either grill or pan-fry the kebabs. Grill over moderately hot coals—about 6 minutes— basting occasionally with the melted ghee.

If you want to pan-fry instead, use the ghee to coat a large, heavy skillet and brown the kebabs over medium heat, turning frequently.

Whichever way you cook the kebabs, make sure to serve them hot, accompanied by the thinly sliced onion and a squirt of lemon.

Tip

Soak wooden or bamboo skewers in water for at least 30 minutes before forming the kebabs.

Serving suggestion: Restaurant-Style Dal Fry (page 147), Paneer Roti (page 120), Green Mint Relish (page 156).

stir-fried beef with peppers

serves 4

Worcestershire sauce? Bell peppers? These ingredients may not sound Indian, but they're well known in India. In fact, the famous sauce started out as a Bengali recipe that was re-created in Worcester in the early 1800s by two English chemists whose names you might recognize: Lea and Perrins. By the way, my recipe is in a style that Indians would call a "chilly fry."

1 pound beef top sirloin or any other tender cut of beef
½ teaspoon ground turmeric
½ teaspoon freshly ground black pepper
½ teaspoon Red Masala (page 16)
1 tablespoon Worcestershire sauce
Salt
1 tablespoon apple cider vinegar
5 tablespoons canola oil

1 pound bell peppers (a mix of red, yellow, and green looks nice), seeded and cut into ¼-inch strips
1 cup thickly sliced yellow onion
1 large green serrano chile, quartered lengthwise (seeded, if you wish)
½ teaspoon finely minced garlic (about 2 large cloves)
¼ cup thinly sliced tomato (about 1 small)

Slice the beef as thinly as you can. Rub the turmeric, black pepper, red masala, Worcestershire sauce, salt, and vinegar into the beef slices and set aside.

Heat 2 tablespoons of the oil in a wok over high heat and add the bell peppers, onion, and chile. Stir-fry until the peppers are crisp-tender. Transfer to a serving dish.

Return the wok to high heat with the remaining 3 tablespoons of oil. Quickly add the garlic and stir-fry until lightly browned. Add the tomato and stir-fry for an additional minute. Add the beef and toss well. Continue to cook over high heat until the beef is done— about 5 minutes. Return the bell pepper mixture to the wok and toss again until well combined.

Tip

Place the beef in the freezer for 15 to 20 minutes to make it easier to slice. Also, slicing against the grain prevents it from toughening while cooking.

Serving suggestion: Wilted Spinach with Red Chile (page 110), Wok-Fried Potatoes (page 104), and some crusty bread.

spicy shell-on red shrimp

serves 4

Here's a great dish for a barbecue where eating with your hands is part of the fun. Shell-on shrimp works best; the shell traps the wonderful sauce and keeps the shrimp from overcooking. Peel as you eat, licking up the juices that dribble down your arm. If you're not used to deveining shrimp, it may take you most of the allotted time; luckily the rest of the dish comes together in minutes.

12 jumbo or 1 pound large tiger shrimp, shell-on
3 tablespoons Red Masala (page 16)

Salt
3 tablespoons canola oil
1 cup minced red tomato

Devein the shrimp without taking the shells off. To do this, use a pair of kitchen shears to cut down the back of each shrimp just enough to reveal the vein—pull it out with your fingers. Snip off the shrimp legs as well. Rinse well under running water and drain. Gently mix the shrimp with the red masala and salt and set aside for 10 minutes.

Heat the oil in a large sauté pan over medium heat. Add the tomato and cook, stirring constantly, until it breaks down. Add the shrimp and all the marinade and gently mix. Turn down the heat to low, cover, and cook until the shrimp are just done, about 5 minutes. You may add a tablespoon or two of water if the sauce begins to dry out.

Serving suggestion: Savory Coconut Rice (page 118), Banana Raita with Cayenne (page 72), Whole Stuffed Okra (page 101).

black pepper shrimp with curry leaves

serves 4

This is a very distinctive dish because the curry leaves and black pepper go together so well. I created the recipe one time when I had nothing but frozen shrimp in the freezer and was really craving the heat of black peppercorns. It's been a party staple in my home ever since, served as a first course with Pickled Cucumber and Carrot Salad (page 71).

6 tablespoons canola oil
20 fresh curry leaves
1 pound large tiger shrimp, peeled and deveined

½ teaspoon freshly ground coarse black pepper, or even more if you like pepper as much as I do!
Salt

Heat the oil in a wok or large skillet over high heat. Toss in the curry leaves and back away from the stove—they'll sputter wildly and turn crisp. Add the shrimp and toss. Add the black pepper and salt and continue tossing over high heat until the shrimp are pink and cooked through, 3 to 4 minutes. Take care not to overcook the shrimp.

Serve warm.

Tip

Try to get peeled shrimp with their tails still on, for this dish.

Serving suggestion: Rice Kanji (page 117), Hot and Sweet Apple Chutney (page 152), Sautéed Coconut Chard (page 105).

coriander shrimp with zucchini

serves 6

Years ago, my husband would eat squash only if it was cooked with shrimp or dried fish, as they do in coastal communities. An avid nonvegetarian, he was convinced that "translucent vegetables" were only edible after the seafood had infused some flavor into them. I'm happy to say his outlook has changed, but maybe he did have a point back then. Take this smoky zucchini dish; once I've added in the shrimp, my kids don't seem to realize they're actually eating squash.

½ pound medium shrimp, peeled
  and deveined
1 teaspoon ground turmeric
Salt
3 tablespoons peanut oil
1 Indian bay leaf

4 small dried red chiles
1 teaspoon ground cumin
1 teaspoon ground coriander
½ teaspoon Ginger Paste (page 15)
2 pounds zucchini, cut into ½-inch cubes
2 tablespoons minced fresh cilantro

Rinse the shrimp. Mix with ½ teaspoon of the ground turmeric and a little salt and set aside.

Place a wok over high heat and add 2 tablespoons of the oil. When it begins to smoke, quickly stir-fry the shrimp until they turn pink—take care not to overcook them. Transfer to a plate and set aside.

Add the remaining tablespoon of the oil to the wok and heat again. Add the bay leaf, chiles, cumin, coriander, ginger paste, and the remaining ½ teaspoon of ground turmeric. Turn down the heat to medium and stir-fry constantly for 1 minute. Toss in the zucchini, cover, and cook until the vegetable softens but still holds its shape—about 5 minutes. Gently stir in the shrimp and the minced cilantro and remove from the heat.

Serving suggestion: Sprouted Mung Bean Salad (page 67), Poofy Poories (page 122).

baked two-pepper sardines

serves 4

I make these sardines over a wood fire whenever I'm in Goa. Almost every household there has two kitchens; the outdoor one has a wood-fired stove that slowly blackens the walls over the years. I love how smoky the sardines get when you place them in an earthen pot on the wood fire with a couple of dried chile peppers. In this recipe you'll make them in the oven, but you could try replicating it over your kettle barbecue if you like.

1 pound fresh sardines
Lots of freshly ground black pepper
Sea salt

2 large dried red chiles, each broken in two
2 tablespoons canola or coconut oil
4 wedges lemon

Preheat the oven to 350°F. Clean the sardines, cutting off the heads and the insides out, unless it's already been done for you. Rinse very well under running water and pat dry. In an ovenproof ceramic dish, mix the sardines with lots of black pepper, salt, and the chiles. Drizzle with the oil and cover the dish tightly with a lid or with foil. Bake until the sardines flake easily—about 15 minutes.

While serving, squeeze the lemon over and pick with your fingers!

Serving suggestion: Rice Kanji (page 117), Spicy Cauliflower Pickle (page 154). Use leftover sardines, if any, in the Spicy Tuna Salad (page 45).

braised halibut
with green masala

serves 4

Fried fish is a lunch staple all along India's western coast, livening up the ubiquitous rice-and-curry. My version uses a lot less oil than the original without compromising on taste. The trick is to cover the pan while cooking, braising the fish rather than frying it.

4 (5-ounce) halibut steaks
Salt

2 tablespoons Green Masala (page 17)
2 tablespoons canola oil

Rinse the fish and pat dry. Salt well and then smear with the green masala, spreading it on thick. Set aside for 10 minutes.

In a nonstick skillet large enough to hold the fish, heat the oil over high heat (or cook in two batches). When the oil just begins to smoke, slip in the halibut and turn down the heat to medium. Cover the pan and cook until browned on the underside—about 5 minutes. Uncover, turn the fish over, and continue cooking uncovered until done—about 3 more minutes. Serve immediately.

Serving suggestion: Shortcut Shrimp-Okra Curry (page 134), Sweet Carrot Chutney (page 151), steamed rice.

pan-fried silky eggplant

serves 4

In my opinion, pan-frying is one of the best ways to prepare eggplant, turning it seductively silky. To make it even more special, I smear the eggplant slices with a zesty spice rub before frying.

½ teaspoon Ginger Paste (page 15)
½ teaspoon cayenne
½ teaspoon ground turmeric
1½ teaspoons ground coriander
Salt

Pinch of granulated sugar
1 globe eggplant (about 1 pound), sliced into ½-inch rounds
7 to 8 tablespoons canola or peanut oil

In a small bowl, mix the ginger paste, cayenne, turmeric, coriander, salt, and sugar. Add just a little water to make a thick paste. Smear the spice paste on both sides of the eggplant slices.

Place a large skillet over high heat and heat the oil. Carefully arrange the eggplant slices in a single layer in the hot oil. Turn down the heat and cook until the undersides of the eggplant slices have browned evenly. Carefully turn the eggplant over and brown the other side. The eggplant should soften but not fall apart. Serve immediately.

Serving suggestion: Farmer's Black Bean Stew (page 145), Lemon Rice (page 116), Beet Raita with Cilantro (page 72).

garlicky pattypan squash

serves 4

There's something about crisp-tender squash in a savory garlicky sauce that's very hearty and satisfying. When I first created this quick recipe, I'd make it several times a week. If you're making it for company, try to find baby zucchini and squashes; they look lovely when sautéed whole.

1 pound pattypan squash or zucchini
2 large cloves garlic
4 tablespoons canola or untoasted
   sesame oil
½ teaspoon mustard seeds
1 teaspoon ground turmeric

¼ teaspoon cayenne
1 large tomato, chopped into eighths
Salt
Pinch of sugar
3 tablespoons minced fresh cilantro

Cut the pattypan squash into quarters. If using zucchini, slice lengthwise and then crosswise into 1-inch chunks. If they're baby vegetables, leave them whole.

Peel the garlic, then smash it with the side of your knife to release its flavor.

Heat the oil in a wok over high heat until it just begins to smoke. Working quickly, add the mustard seeds and cover. When the seeds stop popping, add the turmeric, cayenne, and tomato. Stir until the tomato breaks up just a little, then add the squash, salt, and sugar. Toss lightly with a wooden spoon, cover, and steam for a couple of minutes.

Turn down the heat to medium, toss in the smashed garlic, cover, and cook again until the squash is crisp-tender. Stir in the minced cilantro and serve hot.

Tip

Adding the garlic later in the cooking process makes the dish a lot more garlicky than if you add it to the hot oil at the start of the recipe.

Serving suggestion: Lentils with Curry Leaves (page 143), Potato Raita with Cumin (page 75), any flatbread.

mushroom chile fry

serves 4

When I was growing up in Mumbai, we'd have to drive to the fancy part of town to buy "foreign" produce such as lettuce, strawberries, and mushrooms, all very pricey. Even today, when I'm in Goa, I still have to drive into town to buy my mushrooms, but then I live in a paddy village. The saving grace is, I pay less than a dollar a pound. Here's a quick mushroom stir-fry that always pleases.

4 tablespoons canola oil
1 pound cremini mushrooms, sliced ¼ inch
    thick (stems and caps)
2 dried red chiles, each broken in two

1 bunch green onions, cut into 2-inch lengths
Salt
Dash of Worcestershire sauce

In your largest skillet, heat 2 tablespoons of the oil over high heat and sauté the mushrooms until browned but still al dente. Transfer to a serving bowl.

Reheat the same pan with the remaining 2 tablespoons of the oil, again over high heat. Add the green onions and red chiles and toss until wilted. Transfer to the serving bowl that contains the mushrooms. Salt lightly, add the Worcestershire sauce, and toss well.

Tip

Take care not to overcook the mushrooms; you want them firm, not soggy.

Serving suggestion: Sunday Pilaf (page 115), Butternut Squash Raita with Peanuts (page 76), Pepped-Up Cauliflower (page 102).

gingery paneer with red peppers

serves 4

This gingery, saucy wok-fried dish is an outstanding vegetarian entrée. I use coarsely ground dried red chiles instead of cayenne; the potent, smoky heat goes really well with the ginger. And even if you don't have any paneer in the fridge, you can still have your stir-fry ready on time; it takes barely 20 minutes to make the small quantity of paneer you'll need for this recipe.

2 dried red chiles
3 tablespoons melted Ghee (page 13)
1 large red bell pepper, seeded and cut into
   1-inch squares
1 teaspoon Garlic Paste (page 14)
2 tablespoons ground coriander
¼ cup finely chopped red onion

¼ cup minced fresh ginger
1 small green serrano chile, minced
2 cups finely chopped tomatoes
Salt
2 tablespoons minced fresh cilantro
½ pound Paneer (page 20), cut into
   1-inch cubes

Lightly toast the dried red chiles in a dry, heavy skillet. Let cool completely and, using a mortar and pestle, coarsely pound the chiles into a powder.

Heat half of the ghee in a wok placed over high heat and quickly stir-fry the pepper squares. Toss them around until they blister. Drain and set aside.

Turn down the heat to medium and add the remaining half of the ghee and the garlic paste to the skillet. When the garlic is browned, add the powdered red chiles and coriander and stir-fry for a minute. In all likelihood you'll start sneezing at this stage, so I suggest you step back from the stove and hold your breath until the next step.

Add the onion, ginger, and serrano chile and sauté for 5 minutes. Toss in the tomatoes and sauté, using a spatula to break them up. Cook until the tomatoes are saucy. Stir in salt and the cilantro. Add the paneer and bell pepper. Toss gently until the paneer is well coated with the sauce—about 4 minutes.

Tip

If you have some crushed red chile (the kind that's sprinkled on pizza), substitute half a teaspoon of it for the red chile powder in this recipe.

Serving suggestion: Lentils with Curry Leaves (page 143), Savory Coconut Rice (page 118), Indian Chopped Salad (page 70).

baby potatoes in green masala sauce

serves 4

Whoever heard of potatoes as a main dish? A billion Indians, that's who. In India, the potato isn't regarded as a starch so much as a vegetable, and a hearty one at that. In this recipe I use whole baby potatoes; they're better able to absorb the masala than bigger ones, and they just look nicer in the dish.

1 pound baby Yukon Gold or red
    potatoes, scrubbed
2 tablespoons canola or untoasted
    sesame oil
½ teaspoon Ginger Paste (page 15)

¼ teaspoon ground turmeric
¼ cup Green Masala (page 17)
Sprinkling of salt
½ cup water

Boil the potatoes in enough water to cover until tender but not falling apart. Drain.

Meanwhile, select a skillet large enough to hold the potatoes in one layer. Pour in the oil and place over medium heat. Add the ginger paste and turmeric and cook, stirring constantly, until the mixture smells fragrant— about 3 minutes.

Stir in the green masala and salt. Add the boiled potatoes and sauté until well browned. Pour in the water and bring to a boil. Turn down the heat to low, cover, and steam for 5 minutes. The sauce should have thickened, coating the potatoes. If not, cook uncovered for a little longer.

Serving suggestion: Sautéed Coconut Chard (page 105), Cucumber Raita with Curry Leaves (page 74), Paneer Roti (page 120).

express
veggies

Whole Stuffed Okra   101

Pepped-Up Cauliflower   102

Wok-Fried Potatoes   104

Sautéed Coconut Chard   105

Mustardy Mashed Potatoes   106

Smoky Eggplant Bharta   107

Curry Leaf Green Beans   108

Wilted Spinach with Red Chile   110

Green Pepper–Potato Sauté   111

It's easy to be a vegetarian in India. Wherever you go—from major metros to tiny villages, from fancy restaurants to humble homes—meatless is often the main attraction rather than an afterthought. Ayurveda specifies a largely vegetarian diet, and an entire sophisticated cuisine has evolved around this prescription.

While it's not possible for a book of this nature to give you more than a peek into the breadth of this cuisine, the recipes here feature a variety of vegetables. Although categorized as "sides," some of these dishes are fancy enough to stand on their own, such as the Whole Stuffed Okra.

If you're serving a totally vegetarian dinner, pick two or three sides and add a dal, a *raita* or a salad, and a rice or bread. Alternatively, each of these sides makes a wonderful complement to the main dishes in this book.

whole stuffed okra

serves 4

Every single time I make this dish, someone asks for the recipe. It's visually stunning, and most people who taste it are doubly impressed by how easy it is to make—all of which makes it perfect party fare.

1 pound fresh green okra
2 tablespoons Green Masala (page 17)
2 tablespoons ground coriander
1 teaspoon ground cumin

¼ teaspoon ground turmeric
Salt
¼ cup canola oil

Rinse the okra and dry each one using a clean kitchen towel. This may seem tedious, but it's necessary—otherwise you may end up with a slimy mess in your pan. Using a sharp paring knife, make a 2- to 3-inch-long cut on one side of each okra—long enough to get the stuffing in without splitting the vegetable.

In a small bowl, mix together the green masala, coriander, cumin, turmeric, and salt to taste. Carefully stuff this mixture into the cut in each okra.

Heat the oil in a large skillet. Cook the okra in batches; don't overcrowd the pan or you'll end up with steamed okra and no one will eat that.

When the oil starts rippling, gently slip in a few stuffed okra. Fry on medium to high heat, turning the okra to lightly brown them on all sides. It shouldn't take more than 10 minutes to fry them all.

Tip

Whole stuffed okra can be made ahead of time and reheated in a 250°F oven until warm. They taste great at room temperature, too.

pepped-up cauliflower

serves 4

When there's cauliflower in the fridge, I'll often just steam the vegetable to bring out its pleasant mildness. Or I'll go to the other extreme and really pump up the flavor. Here, a potent combination of ginger and powdered spices does the trick.

1 pound cauliflower
1½ teaspoons Ginger Paste (page 15)
2 teaspoons ground coriander
1 teaspoon ground cumin
1 teaspoon ground turmeric

2 tablespoons water
3 tablespoons canola or peanut oil
Salt
1 tablespoon freshly squeezed lemon juice

Cut the cauliflower into 2-inch florets. Chop the stem end into similarly sized pieces.

In a small bowl, stir the ginger paste, coriander, cumin, turmeric, and water together to make a smooth spice paste. Heat the oil in a large wok over medium-high heat. Add the spice paste to the oil. Cook, stirring constantly with a wooden spatula, breaking up any lumps. Once it's cooked, the oil will separate and the spice paste will smell really good.

Now it's time to toss in the cauliflower. Sprinkle with salt and toss really well; all the cauliflower should be coated with the spice paste. Cover and cook over medium heat until tender but not mushy—about 13 minutes. Uncover, drizzle with the lemon juice, and toss well.

wok-fried potatoes

serves 4

Most people are surprised that I cook potatoes without adding water—but it often works better that way. This recipe is a good example; the potatoes absorb flavor from the other ingredients in the pan without getting watered down. And the onion provides all the moisture needed to cook the spuds. By the way, this dish makes an elegant substitute for home fries at breakfast.

1 dried red chile, broken in two
¼ teaspoon mustard seeds
¼ teaspoon cumin seeds
¼ teaspoon fennel seeds
¼ teaspoon whole black peppercorns
¼ teaspoon coriander seeds
¼ teaspoon sesame seeds

3 tablespoons canola or peanut oil
20 fresh curry leaves
½ pound small Yukon Gold potatoes,
    cut into eighths
1 medium red onion, halved and thinly sliced
    (about 1½ cups)
Salt

Place the chile, mustard, cumin, fennel, peppercorns, coriander, and sesame seeds together in a small bowl.

Heat the oil in a large wok over high heat. When the oil begins to smoke, add seeds and spices and cover—they'll sputter and dance. Once this stops, toss in the curry leaves—they'll get toasted in seconds. Quickly add the potatoes and onion and toss. Sprinkle with salt and toss well again.

Now cover tightly and cook, leaving the heat on high. Occasionally uncover and toss to prevent the onion and potatoes from sticking to the bottom of the wok and burning. Cook until the potatoes are tender but not falling apart, 10 to 12 minutes.

Tip

. . . .

Use a thin spatula to toss; you don't want the potatoes to start breaking apart or getting mashed.

sautéed coconut chard

serves 4

I generally try to serve a leafy green at every meal. So to keep things interesting, I've had to come up with various ways of fixing greens. This is my favorite way to work with chard, which I always have in abundance in the garden. The coconut adds a pleasing toastiness to the dish.

1 pound Swiss or rainbow chard
2 tablespoons dried, shredded,
    unsweetened coconut
2 tablespoons canola or untoasted
    sesame oil

½ teaspoon cumin seeds
½ cup minced yellow onion
Salt

Rinse the chard well and drain. Cut each leaf down the spine, splitting it into two. Stack the halves together and roll them up. Slice into a thin chiffonade. Thinly slice the tender stems.

In a dry, heavy skillet, toast the coconut until lightly browned—this happens within a minute, so be sure to stir constantly or it will burn. Set aside.

Heat the oil in a large wok over high heat. When the oil just begins to smoke, add the cumin seeds. After the seeds stop sputtering, add the onion and sauté until soft—about 3 minutes.

Add the greens and salt and cover. The greens will wilt and cook within 3 minutes. Taste for salt, transfer to a bowl, and garnish with the coconut just before serving. This is equally delicious hot or at room temperature.

mustardy mashed potatoes

serves 4

Bet they don't do this at your local diner. Here's an unusual yet delicious way to make mashed potatoes. The cilantro and mustard dressing make a lovely garnish, so wait to mix them in until after the dish is at the table.

1 pound russet potatoes, scrubbed
Salt
2 tablespoons canola or mustard oil
½ teaspoon mustard seeds

⅛ teaspoon ground turmeric
¼ teaspoon cayenne
¼ cup minced red onion
1 tablespoon minced fresh cilantro

Place the potatoes in a large pan and cover with water. Bring to a boil and cook, partially covered, on high heat until the potatoes are fully cooked and mushy on the inside—they will usually split open.

Peel the potatoes and then mash in a serving dish, mixing in salt to taste. Be careful not to overwork the potatoes, a few lumps are fine.

In a small skillet, heat the oil over high heat. When the oil just begins to smoke, add the mustard seeds and cover. The seeds will pop loudly. When the popping stops, quickly add the turmeric, cayenne, and then the onion. Cook, stirring constantly, for exactly 1 minute and then pour the hot oil dressing over the mashed potatoes. Sprinkle with the cilantro.

smoky eggplant bharta

serves 4

There are variations of this dish all over India, Eastern Europe, and the Middle East. Cooking over an open flame gives the eggplant its characteristic smoky flavor. After it's done, Indians either just dust it with a little cayenne and salt, or take it a step further as I do in this saucy recipe.

2 globe eggplants (about 2 pounds)
4 tablespoons canola or peanut oil
½ teaspoon cumin seeds
¼ cup minced yellow onion
1 minced serrano chile
   (seed it first if you like)

¼ teaspoon ground turmeric
¼ teaspoon cayenne
½ cup minced tomato
Salt
2 tablespoons minced fresh cilantro
¼ teaspoon Garam Masala (page 18)

Wash and dry the eggplants. Use a paring knife to poke a few tiny holes into their skin. Rub 1 tablespoon of the oil all over the eggplants and place under the broiler. Turn frequently so they blacken evenly all over. They're ready when they collapse inward when touched—15 to 20 minutes. Transfer to a bowl to cool.

While the eggplants are cooling, make the sauce: Heat the remaining 3 tablespoons of oil in a medium skillet over high heat. When the oil just begins to smoke, add the cumin seeds and cover. When the sputtering stops, add the onion and chile and sauté until golden brown.

Turn down the heat, add the turmeric, cayenne, and tomato, and stir-fry until the tomato breaks up. Turn off the heat while you peel the eggplants.

When the eggplants are cool enough to handle, peel off the charred skin and save all the mushy goodness inside. It's okay if a few black specks also make it into the bowl; it heightens the smoky taste.

Now add this smoked eggplant to the skillet and turn the heat back on to medium. Add salt to taste and stir gently, breaking up any large lumps. Don't overstir; you don't want a smooth puree. Simmer for a minute, then remove from the heat and stir in the cilantro and garam masala.

Tastes best at room temperature.

curry leaf green beans

serves 4

Is there anything so flavorful as curry leaves? Here, they transform a pan of simple green beans into something fancy, adding an exotic smokiness, while the *chana dal* adds a surprising crunch to the beans.

3 tablespoons canola or untoasted
  sesame oil
½ teaspoon mustard seeds
1 teaspoon *chana dal* (split chickpeas)

20 fresh curry leaves
1 pound green beans, cut into 2-inch pieces
2 tablespoons water
Salt

Heat the oil in a large wok over medium heat. When the oil just begins to smoke, add the mustard seeds and cover. When the seeds stop popping, add the *chana dal* and curry leaves. Within a few seconds, the dal will brown lightly. Immediately throw in the green beans and toss. Add the water and salt to taste, and toss again. Cover and continue cooking over medium heat until the beans are crisp-tender.

Tip

I've specified a large wok or pan for most of my recipes. This is because you need lots of room when sautéing or braising; otherwise, you'll end up steaming the food.

wilted spinach with red chile

serves 4

This recipe may sound basic, but it's got a lot going for it. In my opinion, it's one of the tastiest ways to eat spinach, as my kids will testify. And flash-cooking locks in the vitamins while keeping the leaves green and beautiful. While it's simple to make, watch out: This dish is easily ruined by overcooking, which will turn the spinach an unappetizing gray-green.

2 bunches spinach (about 1 pound)
2 cloves garlic, unpeeled
1 tablespoon canola or mustard oil
1 large dried red chile, broken in two
Salt

Rinse the spinach well in several changes of water, washing off any grit attached to the stems. Drain and shred coarsely into large pieces; I just cut each bunch into four. Smash the unpeeled garlic cloves with the side of your knife to release their flavor.

Heat the oil in a medium wok over high heat. Toss in the chile and garlic and stir until the garlic browns. Add the spinach and salt to taste, toss well, and cover. Leave over high heat until the spinach is wilted but still bright green—about 4 minutes.

green pepper–potato sauté

serves 4

As a vegetable, the green pepper is sadly underutilized, mostly relegated to being a pizza topping. But in the right combination it can really shine; this quick sauté does the job with cumin and coriander.

2 tablespoons canola or peanut oil
¼ teaspoon cumin seeds
¼ teaspoon ground turmeric
8 ounces green bell peppers, seeded and cut into 1-inch strips

8 ounces medium Yukon Gold or white potatoes, halved lengthwise and cut into 1-inch strips
¼ teaspoon cayenne
½ teaspoon ground coriander
Salt

Heat the oil in a large wok over high heat. When the oil just begins to smoke, add the cumin seeds and cover. When the sputtering stops, add the turmeric and stir. Quickly toss in the bell peppers and potatoes. Toss well, then add the cayenne, coriander, and salt. Toss again, cover, and cook over medium heat until the potatoes are cooked through.

snappy
staples

Sunday Pilaf   115

Lemon Rice   116

Rice Kanji   117

Savory Coconut Rice   118

Cracked Wheat Pilaf   119

Paneer Roti   120

Poofy Poories   122

Shrimp Pilaf   124

"Instant" Chicken Biryani   126

What is food, when you distill it down to its most basic level? If you ask an Indian, the answer is inevitably *dal rice* or *dal roti*. While dal is explored elsewhere in this book, this chapter deals with the accompanying rice and roti. Think of these starches as the daily bread of India, anchoring meals in every corner of the subcontinent.

Here I've showcased quite a few ways that rice is made in India: steamed and then flavored, such as Lemon Rice; cooked with spices and coconut milk, such as Savory Coconut Rice; or prepared with dal, such as Sunday Pilaf. There's Rice Kanji, a simple porridge, and an elaborate (yet quick) layered *biryani*.

Meanwhile, wheat in India is mostly ground into flour for flatbreads, and I've included two favorites here, Paneer Roti and Poofy Poories. The latter is a show-stopper; when you're making a poori, it puffs up like a golden ball, impressing everyone around. I've also featured an interesting one-pot dish that uses cracked wheat and dal: the rib-stickingly delicious Cracked Wheat Pilaf.

sunday pilaf

serves 4

My mother-in-law often serves a dish like this for Sunday lunch, because she spends the morning at church and doesn't have the time to prepare a more elaborate meal. Just add the Indian Chopped Salad (page 70) and you'll have a fairly balanced, albeit vegetarian, supper.

1 cup uncooked Basmati rice
½ cup *masoor dal* (split pink lentils)
3 tablespoons melted Ghee (page 13)
1 (2-inch) stick cinnamon
2 small Indian bay leaves
6 whole green cardamom pods

5 whole black peppercorns
½ teaspoon ground turmeric
2 medium tomatoes, finely chopped
Salt
3 cups hot water
2 cups Brown Onions (page 19)

Rinse the rice and lentils together in plenty of water. Drain very well.

Heat the ghee in a large pan over high heat. Add the cinnamon stick, bay leaves, cardamom, and peppercorns and stir. Add the rice, lentils, and turmeric and sauté until the rice is well coated with the ghee—about 3 minutes.

Add the tomatoes and salt and sauté until the tomatoes are pulpy—another 3 minutes. Pour in the hot water and bring to a boil. Turn down the heat to low, cover, and cook for 13 to 15 minutes.

Remove from the heat, but don't uncover the pan for at least another 5 minutes. This allows all the steam to be absorbed, perfectly cooking the pilaf. Uncover and garnish with the brown onions.

lemon rice

serves 4 to 6

This popular South Indian rice is easy to identify; turmeric lends it a beautiful yellow color. Meanwhile, lemon juice adds a fresh, slightly tangy flavor. You can use freshly made or leftover rice; just make sure the grains are completely cool before adding the dressing and lemon juice—the lemony flavor of this dish needs to taste "just squeezed."

1½ cups uncooked medium-grain rice, rinsed
3 cups water
3 tablespoons canola or peanut oil
1 teaspoon mustard seeds
1 tablespoon *chana dal* (split chickpeas)
2 tablespoon peanuts (raw or toasted)

2 dried red chiles, each broken in two
10 fresh curry leaves
½ teaspoon ground turmeric
2 tablespoons freshly squeezed
   lemon juice
Salt

Rinse the rice well in several changes of water. Place the rinsed rice and the 3 cups water in a large saucepan and bring to a boil. Turn down the heat to low, cover, and cook until the rice is done—about 10 minutes. Then transfer the rice to a large platter, gently spreading it out with a fork to let cool completely.

Heat the oil in a small skillet or butter warmer over high heat. When the oil just begins to smoke, add the mustard seeds and cover. When the seeds stop popping, add the dal, peanuts, chiles, and curry leaves. Stir until the dal and peanuts are lightly browned.

Remove from the heat and stir in the turmeric until it completely dissolves. Pour the hot dressing over the cooled rice. Then sprinkle the lemon juice and salt over the rice. Using a flat spatula, gently toss the rice until every grain turns yellow.

Taste and adjust the lemon juice—the rice should taste slightly tart. Serve at room temperature.

Tip

You can make this recipe with leftover rice; you'll need 6 cups of cooked rice.

rice kanji

serves 4 to 6

Served in a coconut shell with a sliver of roasted dried fish, this dish has sustained Goan rice paddy workers for centuries. It's a simple preparation, often cooked during Lent and other "fasting days." And because *kanji* is easy to digest, it's also served to convalescents.

¾ cup uncooked medium-grain rice
7 cups water
1 (1-inch) piece fresh ginger, cut into 4 coins

½ teaspoon ground cumin
Salt
2 tablespoons Ghee (page 13)

Rinse the rice and place in a large pot. Add the water, ginger, and cumin and bring to a boil. Turn down the heat to medium and simmer, uncovered, until the rice is fully cooked and fairly mushy—about 20 minutes or more, depending on the rice you use.

With a potato masher or wooden spoon, mash the rice until it reaches a porridge-like consistency. Add salt to taste, swirl the ghee into the *kanji,* and serve hot. You can pass additional ghee at the table.

Serving suggestion: My favorite combo: Rice *Kanji* with Baked Two-Pepper Sardines (page 89), Roasted Peanut Relish (page 157), and Wilted Spinach with Red Chile (page 110).

savory coconut rice

serves 4

With subtle undertones of coconut, this lovely rice dish is a great accompaniment for seafood. I like to serve it with Spicy Shell-on Red Shrimp (page 86), where the rice provides the perfect foil for the piquant sauce of the shrimp.

2 cups uncooked Basmati rice	4 whole black peppercorns
2 tablespoons Ghee (page 13)	1 (14-ounce) can coconut milk
2 whole cloves	1 cup hot water
1 Indian bay leaf	Salt
1 (½-inch) stick cinnamon	¼ cup Brown Onions (page 19), for garnish

Rinse the rice in several changes of water until the water runs clear. Drain thoroughly in a strainer.

Heat the ghee in a medium saucepan over medium heat. Add the cloves, bay leaf, cinnamon stick, and peppercorns. Stir and add the drained rice. Turn down the heat to low and cook for 3 minutes, stirring the rice constantly.

Shake the can of coconut milk. Open and pour the contents into the rice. Add the water and salt, stir, and bring to a boil. Turn down the heat to a simmer, cover, and cook for 15 minutes.

Turn the heat off, but don't uncover for at least 5 minutes. Uncover, fluff with a fork, and garnish with the brown onions.

cracked wheat pilaf

serves 4

This recipe is loosely based on an exceptional one-pot dish made by the Muslim community in India. The original is a labor of love—whole wheat grains are soaked overnight, crushed in a heavy stone grinder, then simmered endlessly with aromatic spices and a beef shank. My meatless version cuts the preparation time but not the flavor.

½ cup *chana dal* (split chickpeas)
4 tablespoons Ghee (page 13)
1 (2-inch) stick cinnamon
1 Indian bay leaf
¼ cup minced red onion
½ teaspoon ground turmeric
¼ teaspoon cayenne

1 cup cracked wheat
4 cups chicken stock
Salt
2 cups Brown Onions (page 19)
½ cup minced fresh mint leaves
Lemon wedges

Rinse the *chana dal* and leave it to soak in hot water while you prep the other ingredients.

Heat the ghee in a large stockpot over high heat. Add the cinnamon stick and bay leaf. When the cinnamon browns slightly—about 5 seconds—add the red onion. Stir until the onion is lightly browned, then add the turmeric and cayenne and stir again.

Drain the *chana dal,* add it to the stockpot along with the cracked wheat, and cook, stirring, for 2 minutes. Add the stock and salt (not too much, the stock may be salted enough), and bring to a boil. Turn down to a simmer, cover, and cook until done—about 20 minutes.

Garnish with the brown onions and serve hot, passing around the mint and lemon wedges.

Serving suggestion: Cucumber Raita with Curry Leaves (page 74), Hot and Sweet Apple Chutney (page 152), Spicy Cauliflower Pickle (page 154).

paneer roti

makes 10

If you've already made the Gobi Flatbread (page 28), this recipe is going to be a snap. Here you'll stuff the dough with a spiced paneer mixture. It's a bit tricky to fill the crumbly stuffing into a small wad of dough, but you'll get the hang of it after making the first two or three. This roti is excellent on its own, and also will spruce up any bread basket.

Dough
1 cup whole wheat flour
½ cup all-purpose flour, plus extra
   for dusting
1 teaspoon salt
2 tablespoons Ghee (page 13) or melted
   butter
1 cup warm water, or as needed to make
   the dough

Filling
4 ounces Paneer (page 20)
1 green onion, minced
¼ teaspoon ground cumin
¼ teaspoon cayenne
Salt

5 tablespoons canola oil, to roast the roti

Make the dough: You can either use a stand mixer or knead this dough by hand. If using a mixer, set it to low speed, using the dough hook attachment.

Stir the flours and salt together, add the ghee and rub it in well. Slowly add the water, mixing constantly until the dough comes together in a ball. Knead well until the dough is smooth and very pliant—about 7 minutes by hand, less if using a mixer. Set aside, covered with a damp cloth or plastic wrap while you make the filling.

Make the filling: Crumble the paneer into tiny pieces in a medium bowl. Mix in the green onion, cumin, cayenne, and salt. Taste and adjust for salt and set aside.

Stuff the rotis: Divide the dough into ten equal sections and roll each into a ball. Dust a work surface with some flour, and using a rolling pin, roll each ball into a 3-inch disk. Place a disk in the palm of your hand and spoon in a heaping tablespoon of the filling. Bring the edges of the dough over the filling and pinch together into a ball. Dust liberally with flour and roll gently into a 5- to 6-inch circle.

It takes a bit of practice to roll out a stuffed roti without breaking it, so initially it's okay to roll them slightly thicker. Flour the work surface and the bread as often as you need. Keep all dough covered with a clean, damp kitchen towel or it will dry out.

Roast the rotis: Heat a dry, heavy skillet on medium-high until very hot—a sprinkle of water should sizzle off right away. Place a stuffed roti on the hot skillet. When tiny bubbles appear on the surface of the roti—in about a minute—turn it over. Drizzle 1 teaspoon of the oil onto the skillet along the perimeter of the roti. After about a minute, it will lightly brown on the bottom. Use a pastry brush or the back of a spoon to smear ½ teaspoon of oil on the surface of the roti and turn it over.

Use a balled-up kitchen towel to press down the edges—these are the hardest areas to cook. A roti is done when it's golden brown on both sides and has no raw spots anywhere.

Roast the rest and place in a cloth-lined, covered container.

Tip

Place a cloth napkin between the topmost roti and the container lid to keep the rotis from sweating.

poofy poories

makes 20

Properly made, this bread puffs up like a golden ball, generating oohs and aahs galore. For maximum effect, make some the next time you have company. Just remember: Poories are delicious, and even polite guests will swipe several, keeping you trapped at the stove. So follow my example: if there are more than four people at the table, I also make a rice dish. When the poories are sadly over, just whip out the rice dish and announce, "Next course!"

1 cup all-purpose flour, plus extra
  for dusting
1 cup whole wheat flour
½ teaspoon salt

2 tablespoons melted Ghee (page 13) or butter
1 cup warm water, or as needed to make
  the dough
Canola or peanut oil, for deep-frying

You can either use a stand mixer (use the dough hook attachment) or knead this dough by hand.

Make the dough: Stir the flours and salt together until well mixed. Rub in the ghee. Gradually add the water, mixing all the time until the dough comes together in a ball. Knead well until the dough is smooth but stiff—about 4 minutes by hand, less if using a mixer. You don't need to work this dough much. Set aside covered with a damp cloth.

Roll out the poories: Divide the dough into twenty sections and roll each into a ball. Dust a work surface with some flour, and using a rolling pin, roll each ball into a 4-inch disk. Cover the dough balls and rolled-out poories with clean, moist kitchen towels to keep them from drying out.

Fry the poories: Heat the oil in a deep wok or pan over medium heat. Depending on the size of the pan you use, you may need up to 2 cups of oil; the oil needs to be at least 2 inches deep to successfully fry the poories. Wait until the oil is very hot, almost smoking—about 360°F.

Slip a poori carefully into the oil and immediately submerge it with a slotted spoon. The idea is to keep hot oil over the poori at all times. It will puff up like a balloon. When fully puffed, turn it over to "kiss" it a little on the other side. Use the slotted spoon to drain off all the oil and transfer to a paper towel–lined platter. Repeat with the other poories. Fry one poori at a time unless you have a large wok and are fairly confident of the procedure. Serve hot!

Tip

. . . .

Dough is a finicky thing; it doesn't always
cooperate with you and your recipe.
Depending on the flour you use and the
humidity level in the room, you may need
more or less water to bind your dough. So
it's best to work the water into the flour
gradually.

Serving suggestion: Poories go well with a lot
of things. Try Wok-Fried Potatoes (page 104),
Sweet Chana Dal (page 146), Andhra Chicken
Curry (page 131), Maa's Sheera (page 173).

shrimp pilaf

serves 4 to 6

I spent half of 1994 on the road in India, researching local food. Lots of great memories, but this one sticks out. After driving for hours along the west coast of Maharashtra, I'd checked into a little home-stay on a deserted stretch of beach and wasted no time jumping into the warm Arabian sea. When I finally emerged, famished, the lady of the house served me a steaming bowl of this aromatic rice. I've never forgotten it, and here I share my version with you. The recipe requires you to change gears a few times and you'll end up using a few of your pans, but overall it's quite simple to make.

2 cups uncooked Basmati rice
1 pound medium shrimp, peeled
   and deveined
½ teaspoon ground turmeric
½ teaspoon cayenne
Salt
8 whole green cardamom pods
8 whole cloves

1 (4-inch) stick cinnamon
1 teaspoon brown or natural poppy seeds
5 tablespoons melted Ghee (page 13)
1 cup finely chopped yellow onion
3½ cups water
2 green medium serrano chiles, chopped
2 tablespoons shredded, dried,
   unsweetened coconut

Rinse the rice until the water runs clear. Drain very well.

Rinse the shrimp and drain well. Mix in the turmeric, cayenne, and salt and set aside.

Heat a heavy, dry skillet over medium heat. Roast the cardamom, then the cloves, then the cinnamon, and finally the poppy seeds until they are lightly browned and aromatic. Take care not to brown them too much. Peel the cardamom pods and discard the peel. Let cool and powder all the spices together using a clean spice grinder.

Place a large stockpot over medium heat and add 3 tablespoons of the ghee and the onion. Cook, stirring constantly, until the onion is golden brown. Add the rice and sauté until

lightly toasted and well coated with the ghee. Add the powdered spices and salt and cook, stirring, for another minute. Now pour in the water and bring to a boil. Turn down the heat to low, cover, and cook until the rice is done—about 13 minutes.

Meanwhile, heat the remaining 2 tablespoons of the ghee in a small skillet and add the shrimp and chiles. Sauté gently, just until the shrimp begins to curl. Remove the skillet from the heat and set aside.

After the rice is fully cooked, uncover and carefully stir in the shrimp. Cover again and let sit for at least 5 minutes for all the flavors to come together. Serve garnished with the coconut.

Tip

Poppy seeds add a whole new dimension to this spice mix. Make sure to get brown or natural poppy seeds, not the blue-black ones, or your pilaf will look a bit odd. And don't skip the step that asks you to dry-toast the poppy seeds; they'll be almost impossible to grind otherwise.

Serving suggestion: Beet Raita with Cilantro (page 72), Spicy Cauliflower Pickle (page 154).

"instant" chicken biryani

serves 4 to 6

Okay, it's not instant; but for *biryani*, it's a very quick recipe. The popular rice dish normally takes ages: marinate the meat, cook the curry, prepare the rice, arrange everything in layers, finish in an oven. But this recipe is based on a *kucchi* or "raw" *biryani*, where you dispense with the pomp, simply layer the chicken and rice, then set it over a low fire to cook. And, frankly, you won't detect too much of a difference, except that it'll be on the dining table in 20 minutes.

3 pounds skinned chicken parts (preferably thighs and drumsticks)
2 teaspoons Garlic Paste (page 14)
2 teaspoons Ginger Paste (page 15)
2 teaspoons ground coriander
1 teaspoon ground cumin
½ teaspoon ground turmeric
½ teaspoon cayenne
2 medium green serrano chiles, each halved lengthwise
Salt
½ cup plain yogurt
3 cups uncooked Basmati rice
4 tablespoons Ghee (page 13)
2 tablespoons raisins
2 cups Brown Onions (page 19)
4½ cups chicken stock
½ cup minced fresh mint leaves

Rinse and pat dry the chicken. In a bowl large enough to hold the chicken, stir together the garlic paste, ginger paste, coriander, cumin, turmeric, cayenne, chiles, salt, and yogurt. Add the chicken to the bowl and mix until well coated with the marinade. Set aside for at least 10 minutes, while you continue with the rest of the recipe.

Rinse the rice and set aside.

Choose a large saucepan that you don't mind taking to the dinner table. Place over medium heat and add the ghee. Quickly fry the raisins in the ghee—they'll puff up and look like little grapes. Immediately take them out or they'll burn. Set aside.

Add the marinated chicken to the pan and sauté over high heat for 5 minutes—the ghee will separate from the sauce, indicating that the masala is cooked.

Spread half the brown onions over the chicken and top with the rinsed rice. Stir salt into the chicken stock (see Tip below) and pour over the rice. Bring to a boil.

Turn down the heat to a simmer, cover, and cook for 17 minutes. Remove from the heat and let sit for at least another 5 minutes to absorb all the flavorful steam. (Note: If you're not eating the *biryani* right away, keep warm in a 150°F oven; the longer it sits, the better it will taste.)

Uncover, garnish with the remaining brown onions, the raisins, and mint and serve in the pan itself. This is a layered dish; you can't transfer it to a serving platter. Instruct your guests to dig deep to get to the yummy chicken below.

Tip

You could even marinate the chicken overnight in the refrigerator. And be careful with the salt in this recipe—if your stock is already salted, adjust accordingly.

Serving suggestion: No-Pain Green Chile Pickle (page 155), Plain and Simple Raita (page 77).

curries
in a
hurry
(dals, too)

Andhra Chicken Curry   131

Kerala Chicken Ishtoo   132

Spicy Egg Curry   133

Shortcut Shrimp-Okra Curry   134

Green Fish Curry   136

"Irish" Beef Stew   137

Indian Beef Chili   138

Kaju Paneer Curry   139

Curried Yogurt Pears   140

Two-Greens Stew   142

Lentils with Curry Leaves   143

Farmer's Black Bean Stew   145

Sweet Chana Dal   146

Restaurant-Style Dal Fry   147

At first glance, curries don't seem like they'd belong in a quick-fix recipe book. There are so many time-consuming steps: prep the myriad ingredients, brown the onions, make the spice blend, then simmer forever. So is it even possible to make a curry in 30 minutes or less?

Of course! There are two tricks for a curry in a hurry: your Shortcut Shelf and Quick-Fix Indian Pantry. Let's say you're making Green Fish Curry. Your premade Green Masala lets you put the dish on the table in under 15 minutes—basically the time it takes to poach the fish. And buying peeled shrimp makes even shorter work of the Shortcut Shrimp-Okra Curry.

This applies to dals and beans as well. While they usually take a while to cook, I've chosen quick-cooking varieties or canned ones for my recipes. You can cut down even more cooking time by planning ahead and presoaking the dals. And don't forget the ultimate trick of all curries: They taste even better after they've sat for some time, so feel free to make them the previous night.

andhra chicken curry

serves 4 to 6

You'll find some of India's spiciest food in the southern state of Andhra Pradesh. Having said that, I've toned down this (normally) fiery curry for a wider audience. So if you have a higher tolerance for heat, go ahead and dial up the cayenne. Just be sure to serve it with my cooling Plain and Simple Raita (page 77). The recipe itself is delicious; and despite the simplicity of preparation, the results taste as though you spent hours at the stove, so get ready for the praise.

2 pounds chicken parts, skinned and rinsed (preferably bone-in thighs and drumsticks)
Salt
1½ tablespoons coriander seeds
½ teaspoon fenugreek seeds
1½ teaspoons cumin seeds
4 whole black peppercorns

¼ cup canola or peanut oil
1½ teaspoons Garlic Paste (page 14)
15 fresh curry leaves, rinsed
1 teaspoon ground turmeric
½ teaspoon cayenne
2 cups Brown Onions (page 19)
1 cup water
½ cup canned coconut milk, whisked well

Dry the chicken well. Sprinkle all over with salt and set aside. Place the coriander, fenugreek, cumin, and peppercorns in a clean spice grinder and pulse until all the spices are finely ground.

Heat the oil in a large wok or pan over medium-high heat. Sauté the garlic paste, curry leaves, turmeric, cayenne, and the ground spices and cook, stirring constantly, until the mixture smells fragrant—about 3 minutes.

Now add the chicken and mix well. Cook, stirring constantly, over medium heat for 5 to 7 minutes, until the chicken is browned. Mix in the brown onions and water and bring to a boil. Turn down the heat and cook, uncovered, at a low simmer until the chicken is cooked—about 10 minutes. Slowly stir in the coconut milk and simmer for an additional 5 minutes.

Serving suggestion: Potato Raita with Cumin (page 75), Curry Leaf Green Beans (page 108), plain steamed rice.

kerala chicken ishtoo

serves 4 to 6

Ishtoo is the local word for stew in the southern state of Kerala. It's delicious yet very different from a typical Indian curry. For starters, it's mild, not overpowering. And because it's based on coconut milk, the curry itself is pale, with subtle hints of ginger and spices. If you like, you can pick out the cloves and cinnamon before serving. *Ishtoo* is traditionally served with fermented rice cakes known as *appams*, but steamed rice will do quite nicely at home.

1 pound skinless, boneless chicken breasts
1 (14-ounce) can coconut milk
2 tablespoons canola or coconut oil
1 teaspoon whole black peppercorns
6 whole cloves
1 (3-inch) stick cinnamon
15 fresh curry leaves
1 medium yellow onion, halved and
    thickly sliced

1 (2-inch) piece fresh ginger, peeled and
    cut into matchsticks
2 medium green serrano chiles, each
    halved lengthwise
2 medium russet potatoes, peeled and
    cut into 2-inch cubes
½ cup water
Salt
2 tablespoons apple cider vinegar

Rinse and pat dry the chicken breasts. Cut into 2-inch pieces.

Open the can of coconut milk *without first shaking the can.* The cream will have risen to the top—scoop it all out with a spoon and set aside. Reserve the thin coconut milk in the can.

Heat the oil in a large stockpot over medium heat. Add the peppercorns, cloves, cinnamon stick, and curry leaves. Stir and add the onion, ginger, and chiles. Sauté until the onion and the ginger soften and turn golden.

Add the chicken and potatoes and sauté until the chicken firms up—but be careful *not* to brown the chicken. Add the water, salt, and

the reserved thin coconut milk. Bring to a boil, reduce the heat to a simmer, and cook, covered, until the chicken and potatoes are done. Whisk the reserved coconut cream and stir it into the stew along with the vinegar. Simmer, uncovered, for 5 more minutes.

Tip

If you open the can of coconut milk and find that the cream hasn't separated, place the opened can in the freezer for 10 minutes. The cream should rise on its own.

Serving suggestion: Whole Stuffed Okra (page 101), Sweet Carrot Chutney (page 151), plain steamed rice.

spicy egg curry

serves 4

If you've never had egg curry before, you're in for a treat. In India, eggs are the poor man's protein and there are countless ways to curry them, depending on the cook's region and religion. They're also perfect for a quick, last-minute curry, even when you haven't shopped. In fact, this recipe was born of desperation one night with only a can of tomato puree in the pantry, a few eggs in the refrigerator, and four hungry kids home early from the park.

5 large eggs
2 tablespoons canola oil
¼ teaspoon cumin seeds
4 large cloves garlic, minced
¼ teaspoon cayenne
1 cup canned tomato puree

1 cup water
Salt
1 teaspoon Garam Masala (page 18)
1 medium green serrano chile, seeded
    and quartered lengthwise

Cover the eggs with water in a pan and bring to a boil. Keep at a rolling boil for 3 minutes, then remove from the heat. Cover and let sit in the hot water while you make the curry sauce.

Heat the oil in a medium saucepan over high heat. When the oil just begins to smoke, add the cumin seeds and cover. After the sputtering stops, immediately add the garlic and stir until golden. Stir in the cayenne and pour in the tomato puree and water. Stir again and bring to a boil.

Add the salt, garam masala, and chile. Turn down the heat to low and simmer until the sauce has thickened slightly—about 10 minutes.

Peel and cut the eggs in half lengthwise and slip them into the pan. Spoon some curry sauce over them, cover, and simmer for another 5 minutes.

Serving suggestion: Some good crusty bread and a green salad.

shortcut shrimp-okra curry

serves 4

This is a quick and easy way to make a delectable shrimp curry. It's also a lovely way to fix okra, which won't turn slimy even though it's been cooked in liquid. And if you double the recipe, you can serve my yummy Leftover Curry with Fried Eggs (page 34) for breakfast the next morning.

1 (14-ounce) can coconut milk
¼ teaspoon ground cumin
½ teaspoon ground turmeric
½ teaspoon cayenne
Salt
1 small yellow onion, halved and thinly sliced
   (about ¾ cup)

¼ pound okra, cut into 2-inch lengths
   (fresh or frozen)
1 medium green serrano chile,
   quartered lengthwise
½ pound medium peeled and deveined
   frozen shrimp, thawed
1 tablespoon apple cider vinegar

Shake the can of coconut milk well before opening it. Pour the (now) emulsified coconut milk into a medium saucepan and mix in the cumin, turmeric, cayenne, and salt. With your fingers, crush the slices of onion before adding them to the coconut milk (rub a cut lemon all over your hands later to deodorize them). Stir in the okra and chile, place over high heat, and bring to a boil.

Turn down the heat to medium and cook for 15 minutes, or until the okra is cooked and the onion is soft and nearly dissolved.

Add the shrimp and cook for 3 minutes more. Stir in the vinegar, turn down the heat to low, and simmer for an additional minute.

Tip

Don't allow the curry to boil; simmering is okay, but a vigorous boil may curdle the coconut milk.

Serving suggestion: Pan-Fried Silky Eggplant (page 91), plain steamed rice.

green fish curry

serves 4

This is a very simple recipe, as long as you've stocked your Shortcut Shelf ahead of time. But even if you blend your Green Masala specifically for this curry, you'll still be done well within the 30-minute time limit.

4 (6-ounce) tilapia or red snapper fillets,
    at least 1 inch thick
Salt
2 tablespoons canola oil
2 whole cloves

1 (½-inch) stick cinnamon
2 tablespoons Green Masala (page 17)
¼ cup minced tomato
1 cup water

Cut the fish into 3-inch pieces, sprinkle with salt, and set aside.

Heat the oil in a shallow pan over medium heat. Toss in the cloves and cinnamon stick. When the cloves have swelled, turn down the heat to low and add the green masala and tomato. Using a wooden spatula, stir the masala constantly as it cooks for 3 minutes, deglazing with a few tablespoons of water if necessary.

Pour in the water and bring to a boil. Slip in the fish and turn down the heat to a simmer. Cook for another 5 minutes, or until the fish flakes easily but is not overcooked.

Serving suggestion: Savory Coconut Rice (page 118), Wilted Spinach with Red Chile (page 110).

"irish" beef stew

serves 4

Prepared in Anglo-Indian and Goan households, this hearty one-pot dish is quite far removed from your typical Irish stew. I suspect it got its name because it's rather delicately spiced, making it appealing to adults and kids alike. If you want to make it even more child-friendly, just add some cooked macaroni after the stew is done.

6 tablespoons all-purpose flour
Salt
1 pound top sirloin or other quick-cooking,
    tender cut of beef, cut into 1-inch pieces
7 tablespoons canola oil
1 (2-inch) piece fresh ginger, peeled and cut
    into ¼-inch-thick coins
10 whole black peppercorns
1 (2-inch) stick cinnamon
4 whole cloves

2 whole green cardamom pods
1 medium tomato, minced (about ½ cup)
2 medium green serrano chiles, each
    halved lengthwise and seeded
2 medium carrots, cut into 1-inch pieces
1 large potato, cut into 1-inch pieces
½ cup frozen green peas, thawed
8 boiling onions, peeled
1 cup hot water

In a shallow bowl, stir the flour and salt together. Add the beef and toss with your fingers to lightly coat all over with the flour. Carefully remove each piece of meat from the bowl of flour and set aside.

Heat 5 tablespoons of the oil in a large saucepan over medium-high heat and add half of the beef. Toss occasionally, and when lightly browned all over, transfer to a plate. Repeat with the rest of the beef.

Wipe out the pan, return to the heat, and add the remaining 2 tablespoons of oil. Lightly smash the ginger slices with the side of your knife and add to the oil. Add the peppercorns, cinnamon stick, cloves, and cardamom. Stir for a few seconds, add the minced tomato, and let it soften.

Add the browned meat, chiles, carrots, potato, peas, and onions. Stir well, add the water and a little more salt, and bring to a boil.

Turn down the heat to low and simmer until the meat and vegetables are cooked—about 15 minutes.

Tip

Put all the whole spices—peppercorns, cinnamon, cloves, and cardamom—in a square of cheesecloth, tied into a tiny bundle, which you'll remove just before serving. That way you won't have to pick out the whole spices at the table.

Serving suggestion: Serve in shallow bowls, with Pickled Cucumber and Carrot Salad (page 71) and some rustic bread.

indian beef chili

serves 6 to 8

This chili keeps very well, so I usually make a fairly large batch. The leftovers are as enjoyable—add a fried egg on top, serve with corn tortillas and Tomato-Onion Koshimbeer (page 68), and, voilà, Indian-style huevos rancheros.

4 tablespoons canola oil
1 medium yellow onion, minced
  (about 1½ cups)
1 teaspoon Ginger Paste (page 15)
1 teaspoon Garlic Paste (page 14)
½ teaspoon ground turmeric
½ teaspoon cayenne
1 medium green serrano chile, minced
1 large tomato, minced (about ¾ cup)

1 pound lean ground beef
1 (14-ounce) can red beans, drained
  (reserve bean liquor) and rinsed
1 bunch spinach leaves, rinsed and finely
  chopped (about 2 cups)
Salt
½ cup bean liquor or water
1 tablespoon Garam Masala (page 18)

Heat the oil in a large pan over medium-high heat and sauté the onion until golden brown. Add the ginger paste, garlic paste, turmeric, cayenne, and chile and stir for an additional 3 to 4 minutes. Add the tomato, cover, and cook until saucy. Deglaze with a few tablespoons of water if necessary.

Now add the beef and cook, stirring constantly, for 5 minutes over high heat. Use a wooden spatula to break up any lumps. Add the beans, spinach, salt, and the ½ cup bean liquor or water and mix really well. Bring to a boil.

Turn down the heat to low, cover, and cook until the spinach has cooked down and all the flavors have blended well—8 to 9 minutes.

Sprinkle with the garam masala and let sit for a few minutes before serving.

Serving suggestion: Indian Chopped Salad (page 70) and plain steamed rice. Or serve over spaghetti as a twist on the usual tomato sauce.

kaju paneer curry

serves 4

Paneer is the main protein for vegetarians in North India, widely used in Punjabi cooking. You've doubtless tried such dishes as *saag paneer* (paneer with a pureed spinach sauce) and *paneer mutter* (curried paneer and green peas) at Indian restaurants. This paneer recipe is my own; it's a tomato-based curry with *kaju* (whole cashews) that add crunch and richness.

6 tablespoons canola oil
1 pound firm Paneer (page 20), cut into
   2-inch cubes
20 unsalted cashews (raw or toasted)
½ teaspoon ground turmeric
¼ teaspoon cayenne
1 teaspoon Ginger Paste (page 15)

1 teaspoon Garlic Paste (page 14)
½ cup + 1 tablespoon water
½ cup canned tomato puree
Salt
½ cup plain yogurt, whisked gently
Pinch of Garam Masala (page 18)
2 tablespoons minced fresh cilantro

Heat half of the oil in a skillet large enough to fit all the paneer. Quickly brown the paneer on both sides over medium heat. Transfer to a plate and set aside.

Add the cashews to the skillet and lightly brown them, then transfer to the plate with the paneer. (Be careful, cashews burn easily.)

In a small bowl, stir the turmeric, cayenne, ginger paste, and garlic paste with the 1 tablespoon of water to make a thick spice paste. Heat the remaining 3 tablespoons of oil in a medium saucepan set over medium heat and add the spice paste to it. Using a wooden spatula, cook, stirring constantly, until the paste turns golden brown and smells fragrant. You may use a few tablespoons of water to deglaze the pan if necessary.

Stir in the tomato puree, salt, and the ½ cup water and bring to a boil. Turn down the heat to a simmer and cook until thickened slightly—about 5 minutes. Whisk in the yogurt and continue simmering for an additional 2 minutes. Add the paneer and cashews and simmer for 2 more minutes. Sprinkle with the garam masala and cilantro.

Serving suggestion: Poofy Poories (page 122), Smoky Eggplant Bharta (page 107), Potato Raita with Cumin (page 75).

curried yogurt pears

serves 4

It may sound contradictory, but this dish is delicate yet highly spiced at the same time. It will make a stunning addition to your holiday table.

2 tablespoons plain yogurt
¼ teaspoon ground turmeric
¼ teaspoon ground cumin
¼ teaspoon cayenne
4 tablespoons canola oil
2 large Bosc pears, ripe but still firm, cored and cut into 1-inch cubes

3 whole cloves
1 (1-inch) stick cinnamon
1 whole green cardamom pod, slightly crushed with peel on
½ teaspoon ground fennel seeds
Salt

Whisk the yogurt together with the turmeric, cumin, and cayenne in a small bowl.

Heat 3 tablespoons of the oil in a wok placed over medium heat. Add the cubed pears and toss gently over medium-high heat until the pears turn golden brown. Drain and transfer to a plate.

Reheat the same wok over medium heat and add the remaining tablespoon of oil. Add the cloves, cinnamon stick, and cardamom. Remove from the heat and let cool slightly—about 30 seconds. Whisking constantly, add the yogurt to the wok. Return to very low heat and continue whisking nonstop to ensure that the yogurt doesn't curdle—about 1 minute.

Add the browned pears to the curried yogurt. Sprinkle with the fennel and salt. Toss often, making sure the yogurt doesn't curdle. Cook the pears until tender—5 to 8 minutes.

Serving suggestion: Savory Coconut Rice (page 118), Whole Stuffed Okra (page 101), Shredded Carrot Coconut Salad (page 68).

two-greens stew

serves 4

This is my version of Sai Bhaji, the famous vegetable and dal stew of the Sindhi community. After losing their homeland of Sindh (now a province in Pakistan), the Sindhis relocated to India in 1947, bringing along only their entrepreneurial spirit—and their treasured recipes. Today, the community is among the most successful in India.

¼ cup *chana dal* (split chickpeas)
¼ cup canola or peanut oil
½ teaspoon cumin seeds
1 tablespoon minced fresh ginger
1 medium green serrano chile,
   finely chopped
2 medium Yukon Gold potatoes, quartered
1 small Italian eggplant, cut into
   2-inch chunks

2 medium tomatoes, finely chopped
   (about 1½ cups)
¼ teaspoon ground turmeric
¼ teaspoon cayenne
4 cups loosely packed finely
   shredded spinach
2 cups loosely packed finely chopped dill
Salt
3 cups water

Rinse and soak the dal in hot water to cover while you continue with the rest of the recipe.

Heat the oil in a large saucepan over high heat. When the oil just begins to smoke, add the cumin seeds. When the sputtering stops, add the ginger and chile and stir for a few seconds. Add the potatoes and eggplant and sauté for a further 5 minutes. Drain the dal and add to the pan, and stir well for an additional minute.

Add the tomatoes, turmeric, cayenne, greens, and salt and mix until the leaves start wilting. Pour in the water and bring to a boil. Turn down the heat and simmer, covered, until the dal and vegetables are cooked—about 15 minutes. Then uncover the pan and let the excess moisture evaporate, leaving you with a saucy but not watery dish.

Serving suggestion: Lemon Rice (page 116), Shredded Carrot Coconut Salad (page 68), Roasted Peanut Relish (page 157).

lentils with curry leaves

serves 4 generously

After this recipe, you'll never look at a bowl of lentil soup the same way again. Buy the tiny dark brown lentils, not the larger, lighter kind. By the way, the small green lentils from Le Puy, France, will work great in this dish.

1½ cups whole lentils, picked over
2 tablespoons Ghee (page 13)
1 (2-inch) piece fresh ginger, minced
10 curry leaves
4 large cloves garlic, finely chopped
2 medium green serrano chiles, cut into
  1-inch chunks

½ medium yellow onion, minced
  (about 1 cup)
½ teaspoon ground turmeric
Salt
4 cups water
½ teaspoon Garam Masala (page 18)

Rinse and then soak the lentils in hot water to cover while you prep the rest of the ingredients.

Heat the ghee in a large pan over medium heat. Add the ginger, curry leaves, garlic, chiles, and onion and sauté until the onion is browned. Stir in the turmeric. Add the lentils and salt and stir for 4 to 5 minutes.

Add the water and bring to a boil. Turn down the heat to medium, cover, and cook until the dal is soft—about 10 minutes. Uncover the pan and let the dal thicken slightly.

Sprinkle the garam masala over the dal and serve hot.

Tip

. . . .

If kids are going to be at the table, or even adults who are sensitive to heat, cut your chiles into bigger pieces so the diners can easily pick them out.

Serving suggestion: Green Pepper–Potato Sauté (page 111), Sautéed Coconut Chard (page 105), Cucumber Raita with Curry Leaves (page 74), plain steamed rice.

farmer's black bean stew

serves 4

If you were a farmer's wife in northern India, this simple stew would be one of your mainstays. After waking up, you'd place a pot of beans on the wood fire, add some ginger, and let it slow-cook all day, stirring the pot every time you happened to wander by. By dinnertime the stew would be rich and creamy, only requiring a dollop of freshly churned butter and some corn flatbreads on the side. This being a quick-fix recipe, we'll use canned beans to slash the cooking time.

3 tablespoons canola oil
½ medium yellow onion, finely chopped
  (about ¾ cup)
1 (3-inch) piece fresh ginger, peeled
  and minced
4 large cloves garlic, minced
2 medium green serrano chiles, minced
1 (14-ounce) can peeled,
  chopped tomatoes

2 (14-ounce) cans black beans, drained
½ cup water
Salt
1 tablespoon minced fresh cilantro
1 tablespoon minced fresh mint leaves
4 tablespoons unsalted butter (optional)

Heat the oil in a saucepan over medium heat. Add the onion and sauté until golden. Add the ginger, garlic, and chiles and sauté until browned and aromatic. Mix in the tomatoes and cook, covered, until the tomatoes are saucy—about 3 minutes. Stir occasionally, breaking up the tomatoes with a wooden spatula.

Add the beans and water to this sauce. Add a little salt if necessary (remember, canned beans are frequently salted) and simmer for 10 minutes, or until thick and creamy. Stir in the cilantro, mint, and butter, if using, and serve hot.

Serving suggestion: Paneer Roti (page 120), Pepped-Up Cauliflower (page 102), Smoky Eggplant Bharta (page 107).

sweet chana dal

serves 6

This is a classic recipe from the state of West Bengal, where they prefer their dals on the sweeter side. *Chana dal* works well here; it lends itself beautifully to the flavors of coconut and raisins. If you're able to plan ahead, you can shorten the cooking time by soaking the dal in water to cover for at least 30 minutes or up to 2 hours.

1 cup *chana dal* (split chickpeas)
3 cups water
2 tablespoons dried, shredded, unsweetened coconut
2 tablespoons canola or peanut oil
¼ teaspoon cumin seeds
¼ teaspoon coriander seeds
¼ teaspoon fennel seeds
¼ teaspoon mustard seeds
½ teaspoon ground turmeric
2 medium green serrano chiles, each halved lengthwise
2 tablespoons raisins
1 teaspoon granulated sugar
Salt

Rinse the *chana dal*. Place in a medium stockpot with the 3 cups of fresh water and bring to a boil. Turn down the heat to medium and cook, uncovered, until the dal is soft but not emulsified, about 10 minutes.

Meanwhile, in a dry medium skillet, toast the coconut over low heat until golden brown (be careful; coconut burns quickly!). Scrape out the browned coconut onto a plate and set aside.

Wipe out the skillet and return to the heat. Add the oil and turn up the heat to medium. When the oil just begins to smoke, quickly toss in the cumin, coriander, fennel, and mustard seeds. After the spices have stopped sputtering, add the turmeric and stir. Immediately scrape this onto the cooked dal and stir.

Return the dal to high heat and add the chiles, raisins, sugar, and salt. Bring to a boil, turn down the heat to low, and simmer for 5 to 7 minutes for the flavors to meld.

Stir in the toasted coconut just before serving.

Serving suggestion: Pan-Fried Silky Eggplant (page 91), Butternut Squash Raita with Peanuts (page 76), Hot and Sweet Apple Chutney (page 152), plain steamed rice.

restaurant-style dal fry

serves 4 to 6

Most people are familiar with this dal because it's on every Indian restaurant menu, one of those dishes you always order as part of the meal. It's a simple dal, cooked until thick and creamy, then flavored with cumin seeds and garlic. But like many Indians, my family never actually made it at home. So I did a bit of reverse engineering to come up with this dal-fry recipe. I believe it's pretty close to the restaurant version.

1 cup *masoor dal* (split pink lentils)
3 cups hot water
½ teaspoon ground turmeric
¼ teaspoon cayenne
2 tablespoons Ghee (page 13)

¼ teaspoon cumin seeds
2 large cloves garlic, thinly sliced
Salt
¼ teaspoon Garam Masala (page 18)
½ cup Brown Onions (page 19)

Rinse the dal and place in a saucepan with 2 cups of the water, the turmeric, and the cayenne, and bring to a boil. Turn down the heat, cover, and cook at a low boil until the dal is soft, 10 to 15 minutes. Whisk the dal until it has emulsified.

Heat the ghee over medium heat in a medium pan. When the ghee just begins to smoke, add the cumin seeds and cover. After the seeds stop sputtering, immediately add the garlic and brown lightly. Quickly add the cooked dal, the remaining 1 cup water, and salt to taste. Stir, and simmer for 5 to 7 minutes.

Stir in the garam masala, top with the brown onions, and serve hot.

Tip

Work fast when you're dealing with hot fat and a small quantity of spices, as they can easily burn and ruin your dish.

Serving suggestion: This dal goes very well with practically any menu, so feel free to experiment. Or try the quintessential simple Indian meal: dal, rice, *papad,* and pickle. That's dal fry, steamed rice, roasted *papad* (substitute potato chips in a pinch), and any of the following: Roasted Peanut Relish (page 157), Hot and Sweet Apple Chutney (page 152), No-Pain Green Chile Pickle (page 155).

chapter 9

rapid
relishes

Sweet Carrot Chutney   151

Hot and Sweet Apple Chutney   152

Spicy Cauliflower Pickle   154

No-Pain Green Chile Pickle   155

Green Mint Relish   156

Roasted Peanut Relish   157

As if Indian food wasn't flavorful enough already, it's often eaten with a wide range of chutneys, relishes, and pickles that create all kinds of spicy, tangy explosions on your palate.

But these condiments add more than just flavor. According to Ayurvedic principles, a beneficial meal should include the six essential tastes: sweet, sour, salty, astringent, pungent, and bitter. Chutneys, pickles, and relishes can supply several of those tastes. And with such ingredients as turmeric, ginger, and garlic, they can aid digestion and even your general well-being.

But instead of thinking too hard about all of that, just serve yourself an extra dollop and enjoy. By the way, there are serving suggestions throughout this book to point out which dishes go best with each of these condiments.

sweet carrot chutney

serves 4

This chunky chutney needs very little cooking and no curing time at all. On the flip side, it doesn't keep very long, so you'll need to consume it within 2 to 3 days after you make it—which shouldn't be difficult, considering how flavorful it is.

2 tablespoons canola or untoasted
    sesame oil
¼ teaspoon mustard seeds
¼ teaspoon fennel seeds
1 small green serrano chile, quartered
¼ teaspoon ground turmeric

1 pound carrots, chopped into ½-inch
    cubes (about 2 cups)
¼ cup water
Salt
2½ tablespoons brown sugar
1 tablespoon freshly squeezed lemon juice

Heat the oil in a medium pan over high heat. When it just begins to smoke, add the mustard seeds and cover. After the seeds finish popping, add the fennel seeds, chile, and turmeric. Turn down the heat to medium and add the carrots. Cook, stirring, for 3 minutes, then add the water and salt to taste. Cover and cook until the carrots are soft.

Stir in the sugar, cover, and simmer until the sugar melts and combines well with the chutney—about 5 minutes. Remove from the heat, uncover, and let cool a bit. Sprinkle in the lemon juice. Taste and adjust the lemon juice, salt, and sugar. It should taste slightly tangy but mostly sweet.

hot and sweet apple chutney

makes about 2 cups

This good old-fashioned chutney is incredibly easy to put together; just combine the ingredients and cook. Despite the simplicity, I guarantee you'll like it better than your usual supermarket chutney.

1 pound Gala apples, quartered and sliced
    crosswise ¼-inch thick
¼ cup minced red onion
1 tablespoon minced garlic
1 tablespoon minced fresh ginger

3 tablespoons granulated sugar
Salt
¼ cup apple cider vinegar
¼ cup water
½ teaspoon cayenne

Place the apples, onion, garlic, ginger, sugar, salt to taste, vinegar, water, and cayenne in a nonreactive pan and bring to a boil. Turn down the heat and simmer until the apples are cooked and the chutney has thickened slightly—about 20 minutes. Let cool and transfer to a clean, dry glass jar.

This chutney should keep in the refrigerator for 2 weeks.

spicy cauliflower pickle

makes about 1½ cups

When I was growing up, my mother would pickle all manner of fresh produce, so there was usually a jar of something delicious curing on the dining table. Every time my brother and I would walk by, we'd give it the old taste test. Most often this thievery went undetected, but I clearly remember the commotion one time when Maa ceremoniously uncovered the jar at dinner and found it nearly empty.

1 pound fresh, unblemished cauliflower
   (1 small head)
1 tablespoon ground turmeric
1 teaspoon cayenne

Salt
½ cup canola or mustard oil
1 teaspoon black mustard seeds
2 tablespoons freshly squeezed lime juice

Rinse the cauliflower, pat dry with a kitchen towel, and cut into ½-inch florets. Chop the stems into similarly sized pieces. Add the turmeric, cayenne, and salt and toss well.

Heat the oil in a small skillet or butter warmer over high heat. When the oil just begins to smoke, add the mustard seeds and cover. The seeds will pop loudly. When the popping stops, immediately take off the heat and pour the hot oil dressing over the cauliflower and toss well. Mix in the lime juice. The pickle is ready to eat!

Store in a clean glass jar for up to a week in the refrigerator.

no-pain green chile pickle

makes about 2 cups

My husband loves to eat gobs of hot chile pickle. To save his insides from being incinerated, I created this recipe, using mild Anaheim chiles to tone down the heat while retaining all the flavor of the pickle. If you prefer it hotter, go ahead and use jalapeños instead.

1 pound Anaheim chiles
½ cup canola or mustard oil
½ teaspoon ground mustard
½ teaspoon ground fenugreek

1 teaspoon ground turmeric
Salt
2 tablespoons freshly squeezed lime juice

Wash and completely dry the Anaheim chiles. Cut crosswise into ½-inch rounds.

Heat the oil in a large skillet over high heat. Add the chiles and toss for a minute. Turn down the heat to medium, mix in the mustard, fenugreek, and turmeric, and continue to cook, stirring occasionally, until the chiles are well blistered and softened.

Remove from the heat, and add salt to taste and the lime juice. After the pickle has cooled completely, transfer to a clean, dry, nonreactive container and enjoy within a week.

Store in the refrigerator.

green mint relish

makes 1 cup

Here's my version of the ubiquitous green mint relish found on every Indian restaurant table. It's also a vital ingredient in that perennial Indian picnic snack, the Chutney Sandwich (page 169). As a dip, this relish is so good, I've specified it as an accompaniment several times in this cookbook. By the way, my version has a little kick to it, but you can halve the amount of chile if you have a lower tolerance for heat.

1 cup fresh mint leaves, packed tightly
½ cup fresh cilantro
2 medium green serrano chiles
½ cup chopped tomato

¼ teaspoon ground cumin
¼ teaspoon Ginger Paste (page 15)
2 tablespoons freshly squeezed lemon juice
Salt

Place the mint, cilantro, chiles, tomato, cumin, ginger paste, lemon juice, and salt to taste in a blender jar and puree until very fine. Scrape down the sides of the jar often. Although you shouldn't need any more liquid to get the mixture going, it's okay to use a tablespoon or two of water.

Taste and adjust the salt. Transfer to an airtight, nonreactive container and refrigerate until ready to use.

This relish will keep in the refrigerator for a week.

roasted peanut relish

makes 1 cup

This spicy, earthy relish is a staple of farmers in western India, eaten with multigrain flatbread and raw onion as a working lunch. But even city slickers will love its versatility. Mix with softened, unsalted butter, it makes a zesty sandwich spread—or smear the spicy butter on a grilled steak. You could also liven up steamed veggies; first dip your veggie in homemade mayonnaise, then into the relish.

1 cup roasted peanuts
½ teaspoon Garlic Paste (page 14)
1 teaspoon cayenne, or ½ teaspoon
  cayenne + ½ teaspoon paprika
Salt

Using a clean spice grinder, pulse-grind the peanuts into a coarse powder. Scrape out into a small bowl and mix in the garlic paste, cayenne, and salt to taste—you're looking for a rather lumpy texture.

Store in a dry container in the refrigerator.

zippy
snacks

Indian Trail Mix   161

Bombay Bhajji   162

Spicy Fruit Chaat   163

Spiced Nuts   164

Indian Tater Tots   165

One-Minute Chana   166

Rice Cereal with Green Onion   166

Paneer Fritters   168

Chutney Sandwiches   169

As if a huge breakfast and massive *thali* lunch weren't filling enough, teatime rolls around and everyone starts looking around hungrily. You can almost hear their tummies rumbling: *What tidbit should I have with my chai today? A spicy snack, perhaps? A sweet morsel?*

What can I say—Indians love to eat, any time of the day. There's a whole industry that caters to this need, from national restaurant chains to tiny food carts that line every well-trafficked street. They serve everything from deep-fried spicy *pakoras* to salted roasted peanuts. Snacking in India is big business, but home cooks are just as adept at quickly whipping up a snack for a surprise visitor. And most households will have a few shelf-stable snacks squirreled away in airtight containers, waiting to make an appearance at the right moment.

Here are nine recipes to keep you snacking. Indian Trail Mix and Spiced Nuts are items you can make and store. My Bombay Bhajji and Paneer Fritters are deep-fried, but then aren't all the most delicious snack foods? And to ease your guilt, there's One-Minute Chana and Rice Cereal with Green Onion, two low-fat snacks that are equally delightful.

indian trail mix

makes 3 cups

Every state in India has its own version of the spicy mix known as *chiwda*. While it's traditionally deep-fried, I prefer my mother's lighter recipe, featured here. In our home state of Maharashtra, you'd serve this alongside Besan Ladoos (page 182) during Divali, the Festival of Lights.

2 cups plain cornflakes or crisp rice cereal
½ cup roasted peanuts
½ cup roasted almonds
½ cup roasted cashews
½ cup golden raisins
½ teaspoon granulated sugar
Salt
4 large cloves garlic, unpeeled

2 tablespoons canola or peanut oil
½ teaspoon mustard seeds
20 curry leaves
1 medium green serrano chile, chopped into ½-inch pieces
¼ teaspoon ground turmeric
¼ teaspoon cayenne

In a large bowl, toss the cornflakes, peanuts, almonds, cashews, raisins, sugar, and salt to taste and set aside.

Using the side of your knife, smash the unpeeled garlic cloves—not too hard, you want them to stay whole.

Heat the oil in a butter warmer or small skillet over high heat. When the oil just begins to smoke, quickly add the mustard seeds and cover. When they've finished popping, toss in the curry leaves, chile, and garlic. After the garlic has browned, take the skillet off the heat, add the turmeric and cayenne, and stir.

Pour this dressing over the cornflake mixture and toss very well. It will take a few minutes of tossing to distribute the dressing all over.

Store in an airtight container.

Tips

You may use salted or unsalted nuts; just remember to adjust your salting accordingly. If the trail mix goes soft, spread on a cookie sheet and bake for around 5 minutes in a 200°F oven.

Serving suggestion: A tall, cold glass of beer. Or serve alongside Chutney Sandwiches (page 169) and Besan Ladoos (page 182), and call it high tea, Indian-style.

bombay bhajji

serves 4

Batter-fried snacks called *bhajji* or *pakora* are made with all kinds of veggies. But my all-time favorite is the onion version I enjoyed as a child in the city then known as Bombay. The onions are sliced very thin and fried crisp, so the results are quite addictive. This snack is often made during the monsoon season; there's nothing better than sitting on the veranda, watching the pouring rain, with a bowl of crispy *bhajji* and a cup of steaming chai or—depending on the time of day—a stiff whiskey and soda.

1 cup *chana besan* (chickpea flour)
¼ teaspoon ground turmeric
¼ teaspoon cayenne
½ teaspoon cumin seeds
½ teaspoon sesame seeds
Salt

½ cup + 2 tablespoons water
2 medium onions, halved lengthwise and
    then very thinly sliced (about 1¾ cups)
1 medium green serrano chile,
    minced (optional)
1 cup canola or peanut oil, to deep-fry

Stir the *chana besan*, turmeric, and cayenne together. Place the cumin seeds in the palm of one hand, and using your other palm, lightly crush the seeds. This helps release their flavor. Add them, along with the sesame seeds and salt to taste, to the *besan* mixture. Stir well together and then stir in the water.

Using your fingers, separate the sliced onions into individual half-rings. Add them and the chile (if using) to the *besan* batter and mix.

Heat the oil in an 8-inch-deep wok or pot until it just begins to smoke, about 365°F. Take 2 tablespoons of the hot oil, pour into the batter, and mix in well.

To fry your bhajji: Drop heaping teaspoonfuls of the batter into the hot oil and fry until golden brown. Don't overcrowd the oil; fry only three or four at a time. Otherwise the oil

will cool and you'll end up with sad, soggy *bhajji*. Remove with a slotted spoon and drain on paper towels. Serve piping hot.

Tip

Most Indians make *bhajji* or *pakora*, but the snacks usually end up soggy instead of crisp, or doughy with not enough onion. Here are a few tricks to help you achieve the perfect balance. First, slice the onion really thin. Second, add some hot oil to the batter—this makes the batter short, resulting in crispy little fritters. Finally, pick a pot that is deep enough for deep-frying; you need at least 2 inches of oil to make great *bhajji*.

Serving suggestion: Green Mint Relish (page 156) and the beverage of your choice. Goes particularly well with margaritas.

spicy fruit chaat

makes 2 cups

True, Indians will add spices to anything. But strange as it may sound, ripe fruit actually does taste fabulous with a sprinkling of salt and cayenne and a squeeze of lime. Any combination of chopped fruit will do; my favorites for this recipe are strawberries, guavas, pineapple, and mango, or just watermelon by itself.

2 cups cubed fruit (1-inch cubes)
½ cup peeled and chopped crisp
  cucumber (2-inch pieces)
Salt
¼ teaspoon cayenne (or less)
2 tablespoons minced fresh mint
½ juicy lime (or more)

Toss the fruit, cucumber, salt, cayenne, mint, and lime juice together and eat with a toothpick. And imagine you're standing on a hot Indian sidewalk, enjoying a summer treat.

spiced nuts

makes 2 cups

At once spicy and sweet, these nuts are addictive yet wholesome, so I always have a batch at home in an airtight container. Instead of chips, I usually slip a few of these into the children's lunchboxes in the morning. In this recipe, you can tone down the heat if you like, by reducing the cayenne and garam masala.

2 cups cashews or almonds, or a mixture
   of both
1 teaspoon Garam Masala (page 18)
½ teaspoon cayenne

2 tablespoons canola oil
Salt
½ teaspoon granulated sugar

Preheat the oven to 350°F. In a large bowl, toss the nuts with the garam masala, cayenne, oil, salt to taste, and sugar and spread on a foil-lined baking sheet. Bake for about 10 minutes, or until the nuts are just beginning to brown lightly. Immediately remove from the heat and set in a cool place. Once the nuts are completely cooled, place in a dry container and store for up to 2 weeks.

Tip

If you can smell the nuts in the oven, it's too late! Nuts are sneaky; they may not look toasted even when the oils inside have completely cooked them. When I was a rookie in the pastry department at Tutto Maré in Tiburon, California, I'd often be seen running toward the huge walk-in freezer with a hot baking sheet of ready-to-burn almonds. My goal was to stop the nuts from cooking any further by exposing them to subzero temperatures. I'm assuming you don't have this facility at home, so it's best to keep checking on the nuts every few minutes. At the first whiff of nuttiness, take them out.

indian tater tots

serves 4 to 6

Better than fries, you truly can't stop at one of these addictive little potato balls. The bread crumbs in this recipe are optional because it's hard to predict what potatoes will do; once you've combined the mashed potatoes with the egg, you'll be able to judge whether or not you need bread crumbs to bind the mix.

12 ounces russet potatoes, boiled
½ cup minced yellow onion
2 small green serrano chiles, seeded
   and minced
¼ cup minced fresh cilantro

Salt
1 large egg, whisked
½ cup fresh bread crumbs (if needed)
1 cup canola oil

Peel the potatoes and mash well. Mix in the onion, chiles, and cilantro and season to taste with salt. When satisfied, stir in the egg, and if the mixture is too loose, add the bread crumbs. Form into balls the diameter of a quarter.

Heat the oil in a skillet and shallow-fry the yummy little balls until golden. Serve them as they come out of the oil, or they'll end up getting soft.

Serving suggestion: Tomato ketchup and Green Mint Relish (page 156).

one-minute chana

makes a hearty bowlful

Here's the exact opposite of the *chana masala* at your local Indian restaurant. Instead of using a heavy dose of spices and oil, just toss a can of chickpeas with a little lemon juice and garam masala. The result is a light, clean-tasting snack that's full of protein and easy to carry. And if you've stocked your Shortcut Shelf, you can be ready to eat in less than a minute.

1 (14-ounce) can chickpeas, drained
¼ teaspoon Garam Masala (page 18)
1 tablespoon freshly squeezed lemon juice
Salt, if needed

Place the chickpeas in a bowl, add the garam masala, lemon juice, and salt, if using, and toss well.

rice cereal with green onion

makes 1 greedy serving or 2 smaller ones

I have photos of myself as a six-year-old, gobbling fistfuls of this stuff. And I'm pleased to see my kids doing the same. Crisp rice, crunchy bits, what's not to like? Even my kids can make it; it's that simple. Make sure to serve right away, as the cereal will lose its crispness (or is that *crispiness*?) after it's been sitting with the cucumber and green onion for a bit.

1 cup crisp rice cereal
½ cup roasted salted peanuts
2 tablespoons minced green onion
¼ cup minced cucumber
Salt
¼ teaspoon cayenne
1 tablespoon mustard oil or olive oil

Toss the cereal, peanuts, green onion, cucumber, salt, cayenne, and oil together in a medium bowl. You may multiply the recipe as many times as you wish, adjusting the ingredients to your personal taste.

paneer fritters

serves 4

Paneer makes a wonderful fritter. When you fry it, the chickpea batter gets nice and crispy on the outside, while the paneer inside just begins to melt, yielding a delicious molten mouthful. Needless to say, be sure to serve these fritters as soon as they're done.

8 ounces Paneer (page 20), patted dry
   and cut into 1-inch cubes
Salt
1 cup *chana besan* (chickpea flour)
Pinch of baking soda
¼ teaspoon ground turmeric

¼ teaspoon cayenne
1 cup water
2 tablespoons minced fresh cilantro
1 medium green serrano chile, seeded
   (if you like) and minced
1 cup canola or peanut oil, to deep-fry

Place the paneer in a single layer on a plate and lightly salt the cubes. Line another plate with paper towels on which to drain the fried fritters.

Stir the *chana besan,* baking soda, turmeric, cayenne, and salt to taste together in a medium bowl. Add the water, cilantro, and chile and mix again.

Fry the paneer fritters: Heat the oil in a deep wok until it just begins to smoke, about 365°F. Take 2 tablespoons of the hot oil, pour into the batter, and mix in well. Taste and adjust the salt.

Dip a paneer cube into the *besan* batter, coat really well, and carefully slip it into the oil. Be careful of the hot oil—don't just throw in the paneer or the oil could splash up out of the pan.

Fry until golden brown all over. Remove with a slotted spoon and drain on the paper towel–lined plate. Make only three or four fritters at a time, depending on the size of your pan—overcrowding will cool the oil, resulting in unappetizingly oily fritters.

Serve immediately.

Tip

While deep-frying, it's essential to control the temperature of the oil. Too cold, and the fritter will simply absorb the oil, becoming a soggy mess. Too hot, and the fritter will burn on the outside before actually cooking inside.

chutney sandwiches

makes 16 finger sandwiches

No self-respecting Indian would spread butter on bread, add a few slices of cucumber, and call it a sandwich. And no self-respecting Indian would eat it, either. No, there would probably be a request for hot sauce to liven up the bland snack. Here, an Indian cucumber sandwich is pre-livened up with delicious Green Mint Relish. Try this recipe and you, too, may find yourself refusing to make sandwiches any other way.

1 English cucumber
3 tablespoons good, salted butter,
 at room temperature
8 slices rustic white bread

4 tablespoons Green Mint Relish (page 156)
Coarse salt

Peel the cucumber and slice it super thin—if you own a mandoline, this would be a good time to pull it out. If not, use a vegetable peeler to make thin slices. Stack and cut them to fit the slices of your bread.

Spread the butter on one side of each slice of bread. This keeps the green mint relish from making the bread soggy. Next spread the relish on top of the butter. Place the cucumber slices on four of the bread slices and sprinkle lightly with the salt.

Top with the remaining four slices of buttered, relished bread. You may cut away the crust if you like, but it's not necessary. Cut each sandwich into quarters. Cover with a clean, moistened tea towel or, less romantically, with plastic wrap, until ready to eat.

double-quick desserts

Maa's Sheera   173

Sweet Coconut Rice   174

Bengali Rice Pudding   176

Carrot Halva   177

Fruit Salad with Cardamom Syrup   178

Angel Hair Kheer   180

Almond and Milk Porridge   181

Besan Ladoo   182

Cashew Brittle   183

The Western notion of dessert as an indulgence reserved for the end of a meal has always been unfamiliar to traditional Indian cooks.

To begin with, sweets in the subcontinent may be eaten at any time of the day, and in any order during a meal. And rather than being a guilty pleasure, sweets are a part of the Ayurvedic prescription of six essential tastes for well-being, the other five being sour, salty, astringent, pungent, and bitter.

Here I've showcased some of my favorite recipes, for flavor and ease of preparation, but also for their wholesomeness. For example, Almond and Milk Porridge is given to new mothers to help them recuperate after childbirth. Other recipes feature nutritious ingredients such as nuts, dairy, grains, fruit, and vegetables.

maa's sheera

serves 4 to 6

A dedicated scholar, my mother didn't learn to cook until she got married in her thirties—all quite unusual for an Indian woman of her generation. This didn't stop her from becoming one of the most natural, intuitive cooks I've ever known. She tweaked every recipe she learned, making it her own and somehow superior to the original version. Her recipe for *sheera,* a delightful treat with the texture of creamy polenta, does away with any ornamentation and simply lets the dish shine on its own.

5 tablespoons Ghee (page 13)
1 cup coarse *rava* (farina/cream of wheat)
   (not quick-cooking)
2 cups whole or low-fat milk

¾ cup granulated sugar
5 whole green cardamom pods, peeled
   and ground finely to a powder (purely
   optional—Maa mostly skips it)

Heat the ghee in a heavy-bottomed saucepan over medium-low heat. Add the *rava* to the ghee. Using a whisk, cook, stirring constantly, over low heat until the *rava* turns light golden and smells aromatic.

Add the milk and whisk to emulsify. Turn down the heat to low, cover, and cook until the *rava* absorbs all the moisture—about 5 minutes. Uncover and add the sugar.

Change to a rubber spatula and continue to mix, using a folding action. After the sugar has been incorporated, cover and continue to cook—another 5 minutes. Stir occasionally and take care that the bottom doesn't burn.

After all the moisture has been absorbed, use a fork to fluff up the *sheera* and stir in the cardamom, if using. Serve warm.

Tip

To reheat *sheera,* just stick it in a microwave oven for a few seconds.

sweet coconut rice

serves 4 to 6

I spent several years in Mumbai, capital of the western state of Maharashtra, where this sweet rice dish hails from. It's made during the festival of Narali Purnima at the end of the monsoon season, when fisherfolk offer coconuts to the Sea and Rain Gods, seeking their blessings for the new fishing season.

½ cup uncooked Basmati rice
10 whole green cardamom pods
2 tablespoons Ghee (page 13)
5 whole cloves
1 cup hot water
½ cup granulated sugar
¼ teaspoon salt

1 cup dried, shredded, unsweetened coconut
1 cup milk
¼ teaspoon ground nutmeg
2 tablespoons raisins
2 tablespoons slivered blanched almonds

Rinse and drain the rice very well, getting it as dry as you can. To hasten this, spread out the rinsed rice on a clean kitchen towel.

Peel and powder the cardamom in a mortar and pestle or a clean spice grinder.

Heat the ghee in a medium saucepan over low heat. Add the cloves, and after a few seconds, add the rice. Stir gently with a flat spatula until the rice is toasted, but don't let it color—about 3 minutes.

Pour in the water, turn up the heat, and bring to a boil. Stir well, turn down the heat to a simmer, cover, and cook for 10 minutes. Remove from the heat and let sit—don't uncover until ready to mix in the coconut.

While the rice is cooking, mix the sugar, salt, coconut, and milk in a heavy-bottomed pan set over medium heat. Don't let the mixture

burn and watch for crystallization—keep scraping down the sides. Cook, stirring often, until the mixture turns slightly sticky (but is still liquidy) and the coconut tastes mellow and cooked—about 10 minutes.

Scrape the sweet coconut into the rice. Add the powdered cardamom, nutmeg, raisins, and almonds and mix well. Place the pan on a heat diffuser or a heavy skillet and turn down the heat to low. Cover and steam for 5 minutes to let all the flavors come together. Serve warm.

Tip

A heat diffuser is a round, flat pan with tiny holes that you place on an open flame to provide gentle heat to the pot or pan placed on it. You can easily substitute a heavy skillet, or just place the pot in a low oven.

bengali rice pudding

serves 4

There are as many types of rice pudding as there are communities in India. The Bengali version is served during Durga Puja, the great festival of the Goddess Durga. It's simple to make and also one of the lightest, as it uses no ghee. I think it's one of the most comforting puddings you'll find.

6 cups whole milk
2 tablespoons uncooked baby Basmati rice
2 whole green cardamom pods
3 tablespoons golden raisins
Scant ¼ cup granulated sugar

Tip

Baby Basmati isn't actually Basmati at all. The name is probably a combination of the grain's tiny size and Basmati-like floral aroma Its real name is Kalijira or Gobind Bhog, and it's traditionally used in this rice pudding. If you can't find it, feel free to substitute regular Basmati.

Bring the milk to a boil in a heavy-bottomed pan. Turn down the heat to medium and keep the milk at a very gentle boil until it's reduced by half—about 15 minutes. Scrape the sides and bottom of the pan often, making sure no crust forms on either surface. (A heat-resistant silicone spatula works best here.)

Meanwhile, rinse the rice. Peel the cardamom and crush the seeds coarsely, using a clean mortar and pestle.

When the milk has reduced, add the rice and raisins and stir. Continue simmering until the rice has cooked completely and the milk has thickened further—about 8 minutes. Add the cardamom and sugar to the pudding and simmer for 5 more minutes.

Transfer to a dish and serve hot, warm, or chilled.

carrot halva

serves 4

Here's another twist on an old favorite, courtesy of my mother. Carrots are cooked down with milk, fried in ghee, and made special with nutmeg and pistachios. It's not the lightest thing you've ever eaten, but where's the fun in life if you don't indulge once in a while? And let's not forget all the beta-carotene you'll be stocking up on!

2 cups finely grated carrots
1½ cups warm milk
¼ cup melted Ghee (page 13)

¾ cup granulated sugar
¼ teaspoon ground nutmeg
1 tablespoon chopped pistachios

Place the carrots and milk in a heavy pot and bring to a boil. Keep the mixture at a low boil over medium heat, stirring occasionally. When the milk is fully absorbed and the carrots cooked—about 20 minutes—add the ghee.

Sauté the carrots in the ghee for 5 minutes. Turn down the heat to low and stir in the sugar. Cook, stirring frequently, until the sugar is fully absorbed. Add the nutmeg and pistachios. Although best eaten hot, this delicious dessert can also be served at room temperature.

Tip

This recipe makes barely 1 cup of dessert, but that's enough to serve four people because the halva is quite sweet and rich. If you feel differently, you can double the recipe; just keep in mind the cooking time will increase.

fruit salad with cardamom syrup

makes about 1 cup syrup

In an ideal world, every piece of fresh fruit would be perfectly ripe and sweet, requiring no adornment whatsoever. In the real world, sometimes you just need a little bit of something to transform a plain old bowl of fruit into a fancy dessert. This is my way of doing just that.

1 cup granulated sugar
½ cup water
Pinch of salt
4 whole green cardamom pods,
    crushed lightly

Assorted fresh fruit (such as pears,
    berries, grapes, firm peaches and
    apricots, bananas, honeydew melon,
    cantaloupe)

In a small saucepan, bring the sugar, water, salt, and cardamom to a boil. Stir to dissolve the sugar and remove from the heat. Let cool completely.

Cut the fruit into large bite-size pieces. Divide among individual bowls and drizzle a tablespoon of the syrup over the fruit just before serving.

angel hair kheer

serves 4

Here's a pudding that's so simple to put together, yet so elegant. In India, they make it even more sumptuous by topping it with a paper-thin layer of pure silver known as *varq*. Some love their *kheer* warm, others swear by the chilled version.

2 tablespoons melted Ghee (page 13)
1 cup whole wheat angel hair or vermicelli
   pasta, broken into 1-inch lengths
2 tablespoons raisins

2 cups hot water
1 cup milk
Scant ½ cup granulated sugar
Pinch of salt

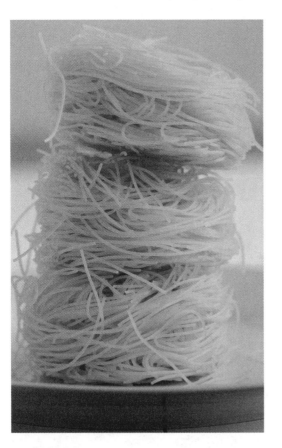

Heat the ghee in a medium saucepan over medium heat. Add the broken pasta and raisins. Cook, stirring constantly, until a few of the noodles have turned golden brown. Pour in the hot water and boil until the pasta is soft—about 5 minutes. Add the milk, sugar, and salt to taste, and simmer until the sugar has dissolved—another 3 minutes.

Serve hot, at room temperature, or cold. If the *kheer* thickens too much in the refrigerator, just thin it out with a little cold milk.

almond and milk porridge

serves 4

Chock-full of wholesome goodness, this porridge has a smooth, creamy texture. It gets its lovely color from the skin-on almonds. Although it's great any time of year, be sure to serve it at Christmas; it has just that holiday feeling.

1 cup untoasted skin-on almonds
½ cup granulated sugar

3 cups whole or low-fat milk
Pinch of saffron threads

Using a clean spice grinder, pulse the almonds and sugar together until finely ground.

In a heavy-bottomed pan, mix the ground almonds, sugar, and milk together, using a whisk to break up all the lumps. Bring to a boil, then turn down the heat to a simmer and cook, uncovered, for 20 to 25 minutes, until thickened slightly.

Add the saffron to the *kheer,* stir well, and remove from the heat. Serve warm or chilled.

besan ladoo

makes 20 to 24, depending on the size of your hands

Spherical in shape and made with all kinds of flour, the *ladoo* is as ubiquitous in India as the cookie in America. This version, made with *chana besan*, is one of the most popular. It's an excellent snack, yet fine enough for special occasions.

2 cups *chana besan* (chickpea flour)
¾ cup melted Ghee (page 13)
¼ cup milk
1½ cups powdered sugar

8 whole green cardamom pods, peeled
  and coarsely crushed
10 golden raisins
2 tablespoon slivered almonds

In a heavy-bottomed sauté pan, mix the *besan* and ghee with a spatula until all the ghee has been incorporated. Place the pan over medium-high heat and cook, stirring constantly, until the mixture smells fragrant and the color is a very light brown.

Remove from the heat and sprinkle the milk all over the *besan* mixture. Let cool slightly and add the powdered sugar, mixing well. Set aside to cool further.

When cool enough to handle, add the cardamom, raisins, and almonds and using your fingers, firmly knead the mixture for 3 to 4 minutes.

Now take a small handful of the mixture, and using firm pressure, form it into a sphere. It's best to use just one hand to do this, otherwise the *ladoos* tend to crack open. Just toss (not high) as if you were getting ready to throw a ball, and press down firmly at the same time. You must use constant pressure while making the *ladoos,* or they'll fall apart in a powdery mess.

Stack them carefully in an airtight container and store at room temperature. If you can resist them, they will keep for over 2 weeks.

cashew brittle

makes about 1 square foot of brittle

Brittle, or *chikki* as it's known in India, is made with peanuts, almonds, cashews, or sesame seeds. Some cooks even add coconut. My recipe balances the sweetness with a pinch of ground ginger, but if you like your brittle straight up, feel free to omit it.

1 cup unsalted, untoasted cashews
2 teaspoons Ghee (page 13)
1 cup granulated sugar

Pinch of salt
Pinch of ground ginger

Toast the cashews in a 200°F oven until very lightly browned—about 7 minutes. You don't want to toast them completely, just to harden them a bit. If your cashews are fresh and crisp to start with, you may skip this step. Let cool and chop coarsely. Set aside.

Using ½ teaspoon of the ghee, grease the back of a large baking sheet (or your countertop if it's smooth and clean). Use the other ½ teaspoon of ghee to grease a rolling pin.

Coat a heavy-bottomed pan with the remaining 1 teaspoon of ghee. Heat the pan and add the sugar, salt, and ginger. Place the pan on medium heat and let the sugar melt, stirring constantly.

As soon as the sugar has melted, remove from the heat, add the chopped cashews, and stir well. The mixture will begin to harden. Immediately turn out the caramel onto the baking sheet, and using the rolling pin, roll the brittle out as thinly as you like. Be firm with the brittle, even beating it a little to flatten it.

Before letting it cool, ask yourself: *Am I a neat, organized person who likes everything perfect?* If so, score the brittle with a knife into symmetrical 1-inch squares. If not, don't do a thing. Now let it cool.

When the brittle has completely cooled, use your fingers to break it either along the lines you'd previously scored, or into random rough pieces.

Eat some and store the rest in an airtight container.

Tip

Don't wait for the sugar to caramelize, or the brittle will be impossible to work with.

last-
minute
libations

Salty Lassi   187

Sweet Lassi   188

Fresh Lime Soda   190

Indian Herbal Tea   191

Indian Smoothie   193

Pineapple Squash   194

Nutmeg Coffee   195

Indian Spiced Tea   196

Masala Milk   198

In India, squash isn't a vegetable, it's a sweet drink—a concentrate of whatever fruit happens to be in season: green mango, pineapple, orange, or lime. Not too long ago, squash was all the rage; when a guest showed up, you simply poured two fingers in a glass and topped it up with cold water.

When guests came to lunch or dinner, you gave them homemade *lassi* or fresh lime soda. At teatime, of course, there was only one thing to serve, unless you were a South Indian, in which case it would be coffee.

Everything changed in the nineties when the government introduced free-market reforms. Along with mobile phones, foreign cars, and superhighways, the middle class got Coke, Pepsi, and Sprite; those humongous two-liter bottles quickly reshaped Indian tastes—and Indian waistlines.

The recipes in this section are my way of paying homage to a simpler time, when pretty much everything you drank was made at home, for reasons of frugality, tradition, or just plain pride. You'll find the above-mentioned fruit squash, plus three versions of *lassi*, everyone's favorite Indian restaurant beverage (after Kingfisher beer, of course). There's also a kid-friendly Masala Milk. And because no section on Indian drinks would be complete without tea, I've featured easy-to-make herb and spice teas that will put their overpriced café counterparts to shame.

salty lassi

makes one large or two 6-ounce servings

Order a glass of *lassi* in India and pat comes the question, "Sweet or salty?" It doesn't mean that you'll find an excess of salt in your *lassi,* it's just to distinguish between the two. I usually drink a salty *lassi* as a midmorning snack, getting my quota of calcium and probiotics; it also keeps the hunger pangs at bay until lunchtime. I've added a variation—fresh ginger juice, which makes the drink even more healthful.

1 cup plain whole or low-fat yogurt
1 cup cold water

A generous pinch of sea salt
¼ teaspoon ground cumin

Whisk the yogurt, water, salt, and cumin together, the frothier the better. Add an ice cube or two, if you like.

Variation

Grate a 1-inch piece of fresh ginger finely and, using your fingers, squeeze the juice over a strainer into the yogurt, then proceed with the recipe.

sweet lassi

makes one large or two 6-ounce servings

If you don't fancy savory beverages, this one is for you. Pleasingly—yet not cloyingly—sweet, it's a refreshing drink for a summer day. Traditionally, it's served in a tall glass, holding at least 12 ounces. The *lassi-wallah* mixes the drink by transferring the contents from glass to glass from a height of 3 feet (I haven't yet seen anyone miss!) to create an impressive head of foam.

1 cup plain whole or low-fat yogurt
1 cup cold water

Pinch of salt
1 teaspoon granulated sugar

Whisk the yogurt, water, salt, and sugar together, the frothier the better. Add an ice cube or two, if you like.

Variation

Peel 1 whole green cardamom and grind the seeds finely into a powder, then add to the yogurt along with the other ingredients. Proceed with the recipe.

fresh lime soda

makes 1 refreshing serving

The fresh lime soda, or *limbu-soda,* is the most basic of all Indian soft drinks, available anywhere in the country and tailor-made for the sweltering climate. Using club soda instead of water takes care of another issue of this tropical land: It's a safe choice at your local street vendor. Of course, you have to disregard small details such as unwashed limes, or hands, for that matter!

1 tablespoon freshly squeezed lime juice
1 teaspoon simple syrup (recipe follows)

¼ teaspoon salt
8 ounces seltzer or soda water

Combine the lime juice, simple syrup, and salt in the bottom of a tall glass. Top with seltzer water. Stir, add ice, and serve instantly. You may adjust the quantity of simple syrup to your liking.

To make simple syrup: Place 1 cup of granulated sugar and ½ cup of water in a small saucepan over high heat. Stir until the sugar dissolves. Remove from the heat and let cool. Bottle and refrigerate for up to 2 months.

Variation

Crush some mint leaves into the limeade.

indian herbal tea

makes 1 cup

My herbal teas are usually made with whatever herb I find in my garden that day. I'm not sure if it's the freshness of the herb or the fact that I grew it myself, but it's an instant pick-me-up. Try this recipe and you, too, may never buy herbal tea bags again. There are various herbs you can use; here I've presented three of my favorites.

1 cup water per cup of tea required
6 unblemished holy basil leaves, or
6 fresh mint leaves, or 1 (2-inch)
length fresh lemongrass

Bring the water to a boil. Lightly crush the herb of your choice between your fingers. If you're using lemongrass, lightly crush it with the side of your knife. Place on the bottom of a cup or mug and pour the boiling water over the herb. Cover and let steep for 5 minutes. Serve strained or just as is.

Tip

The basil grown in India is closer to the spicier Thai holy basil rather than to the Italian variety.

indian smoothie

makes one large or two 6-ounce servings

Most people are familiar with mango *lassi,* since most Indian restaurants offer it. But you can make so many other versions of this cooling beverage, using whatever fresh fruit happens to be in season.

1 cup chilled plain whole or low-fat yogurt
Pinch of salt
1 teaspoon granulated sugar

1 whole green cardamom pod, peeled and ground to a fine powder
1 cup fresh fruit puree (e.g., strawberry, banana, peach, or, of course, mango)

Place the yogurt, salt, sugar, cardamom, and the fruit of your choice in a blender jar and whirr until the drink is nice and frothy. If it's too thick for your liking, thin it out with some chilled water. You may also add a few ice cubes while blending.

pineapple squash

makes about 1 cup of concentrate

As I've mentioned earlier, squash in India is a fruit concentrate that's topped up with chilled water. For the average middle-class, urban Indian, it evokes a ton of nostalgia, bringing back those carefree days when you visited your friend's home and her mother served you a glass of ice-cold fruity homemade squash. If she was a working mom, the squash would inevitably be made by a little outfit called Kissan, now a $5 billion food company owned by Unilever.

2 cups chopped canned pineapple
6 tablespoons granulated sugar

2 tablespoons freshly squeezed lemon juice
1 teaspoon finely ground fennel

Place the pineapple and sugar in a nonreactive pan and bring to a boil. Turn down the heat and cook, stirring occasionally, until the sugar has dissolved. Remove from the heat and let cool completely. Puree in a blender and strain. Add the lemon juice and fennel and stir well.

Store in an airtight jar in the fridge. This squash should keep for a month refrigerated.

When ready to serve, add 2 tablespoons of pineapple squash to a glass, top up with ice water, and stir well.

Tip

I like to add just a pinch of salt to the finished drink to round out the flavor.

nutmeg coffee

makes 1 cup

My aunt, who's regarded as the expert cook in her family, was visiting us and asked for coffee. Not entirely satisfied with the cup she was offered, she whipped out a nutmeg and a mini grater—from her handbag—and proceeded to make her coffee drinkable. Curious, I had to taste it. And ever since, I can't have coffee in India without grating a little nutmeg in it. While we used instant coffee in that first drink, you can try this with your regular cup of coffee. I've found that I do need sugar and milk when I use nutmeg, though, but this is something entirely dependent on personal preference.

Pinch of freshly grated nutmeg
1 cup freshly brewed coffee

Hot milk
Granulated sugar

Stir the nutmeg into your cup of coffee. Add milk and sugar to taste.

indian spiced tea

makes 1 heady cup of tea

While black tea is the most popular hot beverage in India, lots of other teas are brewed for therapeutic reasons. Making these is as simple as infusing hot water with a spice: cinnamon to clear up the complexion, black peppercorns to break a fever, green cardamom to relieve a headache, and so on.

These teas are lovely on their own, but you can also add black tea to make a brew you're probably more familiar with—chai tea. By the way, I wince when people use that term; *chai* is the Hindi word for "tea," so in effect they're really saying "tea tea."

1¼ cups water per cup of tea required
1 (2-inch) stick cinnamon, or ½ teaspoon whole black peppercorns, or

2 whole green cardamom pods, crushed lightly with peel on

Bring the water and spice of choice to a boil. Continue boiling until it's reduced to 1 cup. Strain and serve. You can stir in some honey if you like.

Variation

To make spiced black tea, steep a good-quality orange pekoe tea bag in the hot strained spiced tea. Cover and let rest for 3 to 5 minutes. Remove the tea bag and discard. You may add a splash of milk or some honey.

masala milk

makes 1¼ cups

Often given to growing children as a fortifying drink, this deliciously sweet and cold concoction is good enough to be served as a dessert. Be sure to thoroughly dry your spice grinder before use or else the nuts may start turning into butter. As an additional precaution, I grind the sugar along with the nuts.

5 blanched, unsalted, untoasted almonds
3 unsalted, untoasted pistachios
3 unsalted, untoasted cashew nuts
2 teaspoons granulated sugar

2 whole green cardamom pods, peeled
Pinch of saffron threads
1 cup ice-cold milk

Using a clean spice grinder, pulse the almonds, pistachios, cashews, sugar, and cardamom seeds to a fine powder.

Heat the saffron threads in a small, dry skillet over medium heat until crisp—this will take less than a minute. Saffron is very delicate, so take care not to burn it.

Place everything in a blender jar and mix well. Serve over ice cubes if you like.

metric conversions and equivalents

metric conversion formulas

to convert	multiply
Ounces to grams	Ounces by 28.35
Pounds to kilograms	Pounds by .454
Teaspoons to milliliters	Teaspoons by 4.93
Tablespoons to milliliters	Tablespoons by 14.79
Fluid ounces to milliliters	Fluid ounces by 29.57
Cups to milliliters	Cups by 236.59
Cups to liters	Cups by .236
Pints to liters	Pints by .473
Quarts to liters	Quarts by .946
Gallons to liters	Gallons by 3.785
Inches to centimeters	Inches by 2.54

approximate metric equivalents

volume

¼ teaspoon	1 milliliter
½ teaspoon	2.5 milliliters
¾ teaspoon	4 milliliters
1 teaspoon	5 milliliters
1¼ teaspoons	6 milliliters
1½ teaspoons	7.5 milliliters
1¾ teaspoons	8.5 milliliters
2 teaspoons	10 milliliters
1 tablespoon (½ fluid ounce)	15 milliliters
2 tablespoons (1 fluid ounce)	30 milliliters
¼ cup	60 milliliters
⅓ cup	80 milliliters
½ cup (4 fluid ounces)	120 milliliters
⅔ cup	160 milliliters
¾ cup	180 milliliters
1 cup (8 fluid ounces)	240 milliliters

1¼ cups	300 milliliters
1½ cups (12 fluid ounces)	360 milliliters
1⅔ cups	400 milliliters
2 cups (1 pint)	460 milliliters
3 cups	700 milliliters
4 cups (1 quart)	0.95 liter
1 quart plus ¼ cup	1 liter
4 quarts (1 gallon)	3.8 liters

weight

¼ ounce	7 grams
½ ounce	14 grams
¾ ounce	21 grams
1 ounce	28 grams
1¼ ounces	35 grams
1½ ounces	42.5 grams
1⅔ ounces	45 grams
2 ounces	57 grams
3 ounces	85 grams
4 ounces (¼ pound)	113 grams
5 ounces	142 grams
6 ounces	170 grams
7 ounces	198 grams
8 ounces (½ pound)	227 grams
16 ounces (1 pound)	454 grams
35.25 ounces (2.2 pounds)	1 kilogram

length

⅛ inch	3 millimeters
¼ inch	6 millimeters
½ inch	1¼ centimeters
1 inch	2½ centimeters
2 inches	5 centimeters
2½ inches	6 centimeters
4 inches	10 centimeters
5 inches	13 centimeters
6 inches	15¼ centimeters
12 inches (1 foot)	30 centimeters

oven temperatures

To convert Fahrenheit to Celsius, subtract 32 from Fahrenheit, multiply the result by 5, then divide by 9.

description	fahrenheit	celsius	british gas mark
Very cool	200°	95°	0
Very cool	225°	110°	¼
Very cool	250°	120°	½
Cool	275°	135°	1
Cool	300°	150°	2
Warm	325°	165°	3
Moderate	350°	175°	4
Moderately hot	375°	190°	5
Fairly hot	400°	200°	6
Hot	425°	220°	7
Very hot	450°	230°	8
Very hot	475°	245°	9

common ingredients and their approximate equivalents

1 cup uncooked white rice = 185 grams
1 cup all-purpose flour = 140 grams
1 stick butter (4 ounces • ½ cup • 8 tablespoons) = 110 grams
1 cup butter (8 ounces • 2 sticks • 16 tablespoons) = 220 grams
1 cup brown sugar, firmly packed = 225 grams
1 cup granulated sugar = 200 grams

Information compiled from a variety of sources, including *Recipes into Type* by Joan Whitman and Dolores Simon (Newton, MA: Biscuit Books, 2000); *The New Food Lover's Companion* by Sharon Tyler Herbst (Hauppauge, NY: Barron's, 1995); and *Rosemary Brown's Big Kitchen Instruction Book* (Kansas City, MO: Andrews McMeel, 1998).

index

a

almonds

  Almond and Milk Porridge, 181

  Besan Ladoo, 182

  Masala Milk, 198

  Spiced Nuts, 164

  Sweet Coconut Rice, 174

Andhra Chicken Curry, 131

Angel Hair Kheer, 180

apples, 152

Ayurveda

  on digestion, 38

  on essential tastes, 150

  on sweets, 172

  on vegetarian diet, 100

b

Baby Potatoes in Green Masala

  Sauce, 96

Baked Two-Pepper Sardines, 89

bananas

  Banana Raita with Cayenne, 72

  Fruit Salad with Cardamom

    Syrup, 178

  Kids' Favorite Banana Fritters, 31

basil, holy, 191

basmati rice, 3, 7. See also rice

  Bengali Rice Pudding, 176

  "Instant" Chicken Biryani, 126

  Savory Coconut Rice, 118

  Shrimp Pilaf, 124

  Sunday Pilaf, 115

  Sweet Coconut Rice, 174

bay leaves, Indian, 6

beef

  Hearty Beef Soup with Turmeric, 62

  Indian Beef Chili, 138

  "Irish" Beef Stew, 137

  Red Beef Sandwiches, 44

  Stir-fried Beef with Peppers, 84

  Tata's Frankie Roll, 42

beets

  Beet Raita with Cilantro, 72

  Grilled Paneer and Beet Salad, 41

bell peppers. See also chiles

  Gingery Paneer with Red

    Peppers, 95

  Green Pepper–Potato Sauté, 111

  Stir-fried Beef with Peppers, 84

Bengali Rice Pudding, 176

Besan Ladoo, 182

beverages. See drinks

biryani, 126

Black Pepper Shrimp with Curry

  Leaves, 87

Bombay Bhajji, 162

Braised Halibut with Green Masala, 90

breads

  Gobi Flatbread, 28

  Paneer Roti, 120

  Poofy Poories, 122

  "white" wheat flour, 29

breakfast, 24

  Breakfast Chana Masala, 33

  Comforting Rice and Yogurt, 32

  Egg Roll, 26

  Eggless Omelet, 27

  Gobi Flatbread, 28

  Indian Grits with Vegetables, 30

  Indian-Style Savory "French"

    Toast, 35

  Kids' Favorite Banana Fritters, 31

  Leftover Curry with Fried Eggs, 34

  Spicy Coastal Scramble, 25

Brown Onions, 19

burgers, vegetarian, 46

butter, 4

  amount in grams, 201

  clarified, 13

Butternut Squash Raita with

  Peanuts, 76

c

cardamom pods, green, 6

  Besan Ladoo, 182

  Fruit Salad with Cardamom

    Syrup, 178

  Maa's Sheera, 173

  Masala Milk, 198

  Sweet Coconut Rice, 174

carrots

  Carrot Halva, 177

  Pickled Cucumber and Carrot

    Salad, 71

  Shredded Carrot Coconut

    Salad, 68

  Sweet Carrot Chutney, 151

cashews

  Cashew Brittle, 183

  Masala Milk, 198

  Spiced Nuts, 164

cauliflower

  Pepped-Up Cauliflower, 102

  Spicy Cauliflower Pickle, 154

cayenne, 5
  Banana Raita with Cayenne, 72
chana besan
  Besan Ladoo, 182
  Bombay Bhajji, 162
  Eggless Omelet, 27
  Indian-Style Savory "French"
    Toast, 35
  Paneer Fritters, 168
chana dal, 8
  Breakfast Chana Masala, 33
  Sweet Chana Dal, 146
  Wholesome Spinach–Dal Soup, 57
cheese, Indian, 20
  Gingery Paneer with Red
    Peppers, 95
  Grilled Paneer and Beet Salad, 41
  Kaju Paneer Curry, 139
  Paneer Fritters, 168
  Paneer Roti, 120
chicken
  Andhra Chicken Curry, 131
  Chicken and Cilantro-Lime Soup, 58
  Green Pan-Roasted Chicken, 82
  Grilled Chicken Wrap, 40
  "Instant" Chicken Biryani, 126
  Kerala Chicken Ishtoo, 132
  Red Braised Chicken, 81
chickpea flour, 8
  Besan Ladoo, 182
  Bombay Bhajji, 162
  Eggless Omelet, 27
  Indian-Style Savory "French"
    Toast, 35
  Paneer Fritters, 168

chickpeas
  Chickpea Salad with Pomegranate, 49
  One-Minute Chana, 166
chikki, 183
chiles
  Baked Two-Pepper Sardines, 89
  dried red, 6
  Gingery Paneer with Red
    Peppers, 95
  Incendiary Pepper Water, 56
  Mushroom Chile Fry, 94
  No-Pain Green Chile Pickle, 155
  serrano, 8
  Wilted Spinach with Red Chile, 110
chili, 138
Chutney Sandwiches, 169
chutneys
  Chutney Sandwiches, 169
  Hot and Sweet Apple Chutney, 152
  Sweet Carrot Chutney, 151
cilantro, fresh, 8
  Beet Raita with Cilantro, 72
  Chicken and Cilantro-Lime
    Soup, 58
cinnamon sticks, 6
cloves, 7
coconut, dried, shredded,
    unsweetened, 4
  Sautéed Coconut Chard, 105
  Savory Coconut Rice, 118
  Shredded Carrot Coconut
    Salad, 68
  Sweet Coconut Rice, 174
coconut milk, tips for, 3, 132, 134

Cold Buttermilk Soup, 60
Comforting Rice and Yogurt, 32
coriander seeds, 5
Coriander Shrimp with Zucchini, 88
Corn Salad with Cracked Pepper, 48
cream of wheat, 8
  Maa's Sheera, 173
cucumber
  Cucumber Raita with Curry
    Leaves, 74
  Pickled Cucumber and Carrot
    Salad, 71
  Spicy Fruit Chaat, 163
cumin seeds, 5
  Potato Raita with Cumin, 75
curries
  Andhra Chicken Curry, 131
  Curried Yogurt Pears, 140
  Green Fish Curry, 136
  Indian Beef Chili, 138
  Kaju Paneer Curry, 139
  Kerala Chicken Ishtoo, 132
  Lentils with Curry Leaves, 143
  Shortcut Shrimp-Okra Curry, 134
  Spicy Egg Curry, 133
  Two-Greens Stew, 142
curry leaves, fresh, 8
  Black Pepper Shrimp with Curry
    Leaves, 87
  Cucumber Raita with Curry
    Leaves, 74
  Curry Leaf Green Beans, 108

d

dals, 3, 8
  Breakfast Chana Masala, 33
  Restaurant-Style Dal Fry, 147
  Sweet Chana Dal, 146
  Wholesome Spinach–Dal Soup, 57
desserts
  Almond and Milk Porridge, 181
  Angel Hair Kheer, 180
  Bengali Rice Pudding, 176
  Besan Ladoo, 182
  Carrot Halva, 177
  Cashew Brittle, 183
  Fruit Salad with Cardamom
    Syrup, 178
  Maa's Sheera, 173
  Sweet Coconut Rice, 174
  tradition for sweets, 172
digestion, 38
dinner, 102
  Andhra Chicken Curry, 131
  Baby Potatoes in Green Masala
    Sauce, 96
  Baked Two-Pepper Sardines, 89
  Black Pepper Shrimp with Curry
    Leaves, 87
  Braised Halibut with Green Masala,
    90
  Chicken and Cilantro-Lime Soup, 58
  Coriander Shrimp with Zucchini, 88
  Garlicky Pattypan Squash, 92
  Gingery Paneer with Red
    Peppers, 95
  Green Pan-Roasted Chicken, 82
  Grilled Chicken Wrap, 40
  Hearty Beef Soup with Turmeric, 62
  Indian Beef Chili, 138
  Indian Veggie Burger, 46
  "Instant" Chicken Biryani, 126
  "Irish" Beef Stew, 137
  Kerala Chicken Ishtoo, 132
  Lamb Seekh Kebabs, 83

  Mushroom Chile Fry, 94
  Pan-Fried Silky Eggplant, 91
  Red Beef Sandwiches, 44
  Red Braised Chicken, 81
  Spicy Shell-on Red Shrimp, 86
  Stir-fried Beef with Peppers, 84
  Tata's Frankie Roll, 42
  vegetarian, 46, 100, 139
drinks
  Fresh Lime Soda, 190
  Indian Herbal Tea, 191
  Indian Smoothie, 193
  Indian Spiced Tea, 196
  Masala Milk, 198
  Nutmeg Coffee, 195
  Pineapple Squash, 194
  Salty Lassi, 187
  Sweet Lassi, 188

e

Egg Roll, 26
Eggless Omelet, 27
eggplant
  Pan-Fried Silky Eggplant, 91
  Smoky Eggplant Bharta, 107
eggs
  Egg Roll, 26
  Leftover Curry with Fried Eggs, 34
  Spicy Coastal Scramble, 25
  Spicy Egg Curry, 133

f

farina, 8
  Maa's Sheera, 173
fennel seeds, 6
fenugreek seeds, 6
fish. See also seafood
  Baked Two-Pepper Sardines, 89
  Braised Halibut with Green
    Masala, 90
  Green Fish Curry, 136
  Spicy Tuna Salad, 45

flatbreads
  Gobi Flatbread, 28
  Paneer Roti, 120
  Poofy Poories, 122
  "white" wheat flour, 29
flour, 3, 8. See also chickpea flour
  amount in grams, 201
  "white" wheat flour, 29
freezer, 4
Fresh Lime Soda, 190
fridge, 4
fruit
  Banana Raita with Cayenne, 72
  Chicken and Cilantro-Lime Soup, 58
  Chickpea Salad with Pomegranate,
    49
  Curried Yogurt Pears, 140
  drinks, 186
  Fresh Lime Soda, 190
  Fruit Salad with Cardamom
    Syrup, 178
  Hot and Sweet Apple Chutney, 152
  Indian Smoothie, 193
  Kids' Favorite Banana Fritters, 31
  Lemon Rice, 116
  Pineapple Squash, 194
  Spicy Fruit Chaat, 163

g

Garam Masala, 18
Garlic Paste, 14
Garlicky Pattypan Squash, 92
Ghee, homemade, 13
ginger
  fresh, 95
  Ginger Paste, 15
  Gingery Paneer with Red
    Peppers, 95
Gobi Flatbread, 28
Green Fish Curry, 136

Green Masala
  Baby Potatoes in Green Masala
    Sauce, 96
  Braised Halibut with Green
    Masala, 90
  homemade, 17
Green Mint Relish, 156
green mung beans, 8, 67
Green Pan-Roasted Chicken, 82
Green Pepper–Potato Sauté, 111
Grilled Chicken Wrap, 40
Grilled Paneer and Beet Salad, 41
grits, 30

h

Hearty Beef Soup with Turmeric, 62
herbs, 8
holy basil, 191
Hot and Sweet Apple Chutney, 152

i

Incendiary Pepper Water, 56
Indian-style
  Indian Beef Chili, 138
  Indian Chopped Salad, 70
  Indian Grits with Vegetables, 30
  Indian Herbal Tea, 191
  Indian Smoothie, 193
  Indian Spiced Tea, 196
  Indian Tater Tots, 165
  Indian Trail Mix, 161
  Indian Veggie Burger, 46
  Indian-Style Savory "French"
    Toast, 35
ingredient equivalents, in grams, 201
"Instant" Chicken Biryani, 126
"Irish" Beef Stew, 137

k

Kaju Paneer Curry, 139
Kerala Chicken Ishtoo, 132

kids
  Bombay Bhajji, 162
  Chicken and Cilantro-Lime Soup, 58
  Comforting Rice and Yogurt, 32
  Hearty Beef Soup with Turmeric, 62
  Indian Chopped Salad, 70
  Indian Grits with Vegetables, 30
  Indian Smoothie, 193
  Indian Tater Tots, 165
  Indian Trail Mix, 161
  "Irish" Beef Stew, 137
  Kids' Favorite Banana Fritters, 31
  Lentils with Curry Leaves, 143
  Masala Milk, 198
  Minestrone for Mira, 61
  Red Beef Sandwiches, 44
  Rice Cereal with Green Onion, 166
  Spiced Nuts, 164
  Spicy Egg Curry, 133
  Wilted Spinach with Red Chile, 110

l

Lamb Seekh Kebabs, 83
lassi
  Salty Lassi, 187
  Sweet Lassi, 188
Leftover Curry with Fried Eggs, 34
lemongrass, 191
lentils, 8. See also dals
  Lentils with Curry Leaves, 143
lime
  Chicken and Cilantro-Lime Soup, 58
  Fresh Lime Soda, 190
lunch
  Chickpea Salad with Pomegranate,
    49
  Corn Salad with Cracked Pepper, 48
  Grilled Chicken Wrap, 40
  Grilled Paneer and Beet Salad, 41
  Indian Veggie Burger, 46
  Potato "Chops," 39
  Red Beef Sandwiches, 44
  A Spicy Bowl of Peas, 50

Spicy Tuna Salad, 45
Tata's Frankie Roll, 42

m

Maa's Sheera, 173
main dishes
  Andhra Chicken Curry, 131
  Baby Potatoes in Green Masala
    Sauce, 96
  Baked Two-Pepper Sardines, 89
  Black Pepper Shrimp with Curry
    Leaves, 87
  Braised Halibut with Green Masala,
    90
  Chicken and Cilantro-Lime Soup, 58
  Coriander Shrimp with Zucchini, 88
  Garlicky Pattypan Squash, 92
  Gingery Paneer with Red Peppers,
    95
  Green Pan-Roasted Chicken, 82
  Grilled Chicken Wrap, 40
  Hearty Beef Soup with Turmeric, 62
  Indian Beef Chili, 138
  "Instant" Chicken Biryani, 126
  "Irish" Beef Stew, 137
  Kerala Chicken Ishtoo, 132
  Lamb Seekh Kebabs, 83
  Mushroom Chile Fry, 94
  Pan-Fried Silky Eggplant, 91
  Red Beef Sandwiches, 44
  Red Braised Chicken, 81
  Spicy Shell-on Red Shrimp, 86
  Stir-fried Beef with Peppers, 84
  Tata's Frankie Roll, 42
masala
  Baby Potatoes in Green Masala
    Sauce, 96
  Braised Halibut with Green
    Masala, 90
  Green Masala, 17
  Masala Milk, 198
  Red Masala, 16

masoor dal, 3, 8
   Minestrone for Mira, 61
   Restaurant-Style Dal Fry, 147
   Sunday Pilaf, 115
meat dishes
   Andhra Chicken Curry, 131
   Chicken and Cilantro-Lime Soup, 58
   Green Pan-Roasted Chicken, 82
   Grilled Chicken Wrap, 40
   Hearty Beef Soup with Turmeric, 62
   Indian Beef Chili, 138
   "Instant" Chicken Biryani, 126
   "Irish" Beef Stew, 137
   Kerala Chicken Ishtoo, 132
   Lamb Seekh Kebabs, 83
   Red Beef Sandwiches, 44
   Red Braised Chicken, 81
   Stir-fried Beef with Peppers, 84
   Tata's Frankie Roll, 42
metric conversions and equivalents, 199–200
milk. See also coconut milk, tips for
   Almond and Milk Porridge, 181
   Cold Buttermilk Soup, 60
   Masala Milk, 198
Minestrone for Mira, 61
mint
   Chutney Sandwiches, 169
   Green Mint Relish, 156
   Indian Herbal Tea, 191
mung dal, green, 8
   Sprouted Mung Bean Salad, 67
Mushroom Chile Fry, 94
mustard seeds, 5
Mustardy Mashed Potatoes, 106

n
No-Pain Green Chile Pickle, 155
nutmeg, 6
   Nutmeg Coffee, 195

nuts, 4
   Almond and Milk Porridge, 181
   Besan Ladoo, 182
   Butternut Squash Raita with Peanuts, 76
   Carrot Halva, 177
   Cashew Brittle, 183
   Indian Trail Mix, 161
   Masala Milk, 198
   Roasted Peanut Relish, 157
   Spiced Nuts, 164
   Sweet Coconut Rice, 174

o
oils, 7
okra
   Shortcut Shrimp-Okra Curry, 134
   Whole Stuffed Okra, 101
omelet
   with eggs, 26
   without eggs, 27
One-Minute Chana, 166
onions
   Bombay Bhajji, 162
   Brown Onions, 19
   Tomato and Onion Koshimbeer, 68
oven temperatures, 201

p
pakora, 162
paneer
   Gingery Paneer with Red Peppers, 95
   Grilled Paneer and Beet Salad, 41
   homemade, 20
   Kaju Paneer Curry, 139
   Paneer Fritters, 168
   Paneer Roti, 120
Pan-Fried Silky Eggplant, 91
party foods. See special occasions
pattypan squash, 92

peanuts
   Butternut Squash Raita with Peanuts, 76
   Roasted Peanut Relish, 157
pears
   Curried Yogurt Pears, 140
   Fruit Salad with Cardamom Syrup, 178
peppercorns, 5
peppers, bell. See also chiles
   Gingery Paneer with Red Peppers, 95
   Green Pepper–Potato Sauté, 111
   Stir-fried Beef with Peppers, 84
Pickled Cucumber and Carrot Salad, 71
pickles
   No-Pain Green Chile Pickle, 155
   Pickled Cucumber and Carrot Salad, 71
   Spicy Cauliflower Pickle, 154
pilaf
   Shrimp Pilaf, 124
   Sunday Pilaf, 115
Pineapple Squash, 194
pink lentils. See masoor dal
pistachios, 4
   Masala Milk, 198
Plain and Simple Raita, 77
pomegranate, 49
Poofy Poories, 122
porridge, 181
potato
   Baby Potatoes in Green Masala Sauce, 96
   Green Pepper–Potato Sauté, 111
   Indian Tater Tots, 165
   Mustardy Mashed Potatoes, 106
   Potato "Chops," 39
   Potato Raita with Cumin, 75
   Wok-Fried Potatoes, 104

r

raita, 38
   Banana Raita with Cayenne, 72
   Beet Raita with Cilantro, 72
   Butternut Squash Raita with
      Peanuts, 76
   Cucumber Raita with Curry
      Leaves, 74
   Plain and Simple Raita, 77
   Potato Raita with Cumin, 75
Red Beef Sandwiches, 44
Red Braised Chicken, 81
Red Masala, 16
relishes
   Green Mint Relish, 156
   Hot and Sweet Apple Chutney, 152
   No-Pain Green Chile Pickle, 155
   Spicy Cauliflower Pickle, 154
   Sweet Carrot Chutney, 151
Restaurant-Style Dal Fry, 147
rice, 3, 7
   amount in grams, 201
   Bengali Rice Pudding, 176
   Comforting Rice and Yogurt, 32
   "Instant" Chicken Biryani, 126
   Lemon Rice, 116
   Rice Cereal with Green Onion, 166
   Rice Kanji, 117
   Savory Coconut Rice, 118
   Shrimp Pilaf, 124
   Sunday Pilaf, 115
   Sweet Coconut Rice, 174

s

saffron, 7
   Almond and Milk Porridge, 181
   Masala Milk, 198
salads
   Banana Raita with Cayenne, 72
   Beet Raita with Cilantro, 72
   Butternut Squash Raita with
      Peanuts, 76

   Chickpea Salad with Pomegranate,
      49
   Corn Salad with Cracked Pepper, 48
   Cucumber Raita with Curry
      Leaves, 74
   Grilled Paneer and Beet Salad, 41
   Indian Chopped Salad, 70
   Pickled Cucumber and Carrot
      Salad, 71
   Plain and Simple Raita, 77
   Potato Raita with Cumin, 75
   Shredded Carrot Coconut Salad, 68
   Spicy Tuna Salad, 45
   Sprouted Mung Bean Salad, 67
   Tomato and Onion Koshimbeer, 68
salt, 7
Salty Lassi, 187
sandwiches
   Chutney Sandwiches, 169
   Grilled Chicken Wrap, 40
   Indian Veggie Burger, 46
   Red Beef Sandwiches, 44
Sautéed Coconut Chard, 105
Savory Coconut Rice, 118
seafood
   Baked Two-Pepper Sardines, 89
   Black Pepper Shrimp with Curry
      Leaves, 87
   Braised Halibut with Green
      Masala, 90
   Coriander Shrimp with Zucchini, 88
   Green Fish Curry, 136
   Shortcut Shrimp-Okra Curry, 134
   Shrimp Pilaf, 124
   Spicy Shell-on Red Shrimp, 86
   Spicy Tuna Salad, 45
seeds, 4, 5, 6. See also nuts
   Bombay Bhajji, 162
   Potato Raita with Cumin, 75
serrano chiles, 8

shopping list, 3–4
   demystified, 5–9
shortcut shelf, 12
   Brown Onions, 19
   Garam Masala, 18
   Garlic Paste, 14
   Ghee, 13
   Ginger Paste, 15
   Green Masala, 17
   Paneer, 20
   Red Masala, 16
Shortcut Shrimp-Okra Curry, 134
Shredded Carrot Coconut Salad, 68
shrimp. See also seafood
   Black Pepper Shrimp with Curry
      Leaves, 87
   Coriander Shrimp with Zucchini, 88
   Shortcut Shrimp-Okra Curry, 134
   Shrimp Pilaf, 124
   Spicy Shell-on Red Shrimp, 86
snacks
   Bombay Bhajji, 162
   Chutney Sandwiches, 169
   Indian Tater Tots, 165
   Indian Trail Mix, 161
   One-Minute Chana, 166
   Paneer Fritters, 168
   Rice Cereal with Green Onion, 166
   Spiced Nuts, 164
   Spicy Fruit Chaat, 163
soups
   Chicken and Cilantro–Lime Soup, 58
   Cold Buttermilk Soup, 60
   Hearty Beef Soup with Turmeric, 62
   Incendiary Pepper Water, 56
   Minestrone for Mira, 61
   Tomato Water, 55
   Wholesome Spinach–Dal Soup, 57
special occasions
   Andhra Chicken Curry, 131
   Angel Hair Kheer, 180
   Bengali Rice Pudding, 176

special occasions (*continued*)

    Besan Ladoo, 182

    beverages for, 186

    Black Pepper Shrimp with Curry Leaves, 87

    Braised Halibut with Green Masala, 90

    Carrot Halva, 177

    Green Pan-Roasted Chicken, 82

    "Instant" Chicken Biryani, 126

    Kerala Chicken Ishtoo, 132

    Lamb Seekh Kebabs, 83

    Pan-Fried Silky Eggplant, 91

    Poofy Poories, 122

    Potato "Chops," 39

    Potato Raita with Cumin, 75

    Red Braised Chicken, 81

    Stir-fried Beef with Peppers, 84

    Whole Stuffed Okra, 101

Spiced Nuts, 164

spices, 3, 5–7

    Garam Masala, 18

A Spicy Bowl of Peas, 50

Spicy Cauliflower Pickle, 154

Spicy Coastal Scramble, 25

Spicy Egg Curry, 133

Spicy Fruit Chaat, 163

Spicy Shell-on Red Shrimp, 86

Spicy Tuna Salad, 45

spinach

    Two-Greens Stew, 142

    Wholesome Spinach–Dal Soup, 57

    Wilted Spinach with Red Chile, 110

Sprouted Mung Bean Salad, 67

squash

    Butternut Squash Raita with Peanuts, 76

    Coriander Shrimp with Zucchini, 88

    Garlicky Pattypan Squash, 92

squash, fruit, 186

    Pineapple Squash, 194

Stir-fried Beef with Peppers, 84

sugar, amount in grams, 201

Sunday Pilaf, 115

Sweet Carrot Chutney, 151

Sweet Coconut Rice, 174

Sweet Lassi, 188

t

Tata's Frankie Roll, 42

tea

    Indian Herbal Tea, 191

    Indian Spiced Tea, 196

thali, 38, 160

tomatoes

    Tomato and Onion Koshimbeer, 68

    Tomato Water, 55

turmeric, 5

    Hearty Beef Soup with Turmeric, 62

Two-Greens Stew, 142

v

vegetable dishes

    Beet Raita with Cilantro, 72

    Butternut Squash Raita with Peanuts, 76

    Coriander Shrimp with Zucchini, 88

    Corn Salad with Cracked Pepper, 48

    Cucumber Raita with Curry Leaves, 74

    Curry Leaf Green Beans, 108

    Garlicky Pattypan Squash, 92

    Green Pepper–Potato Sauté, 111

    Grilled Paneer and Beet Salad, 41

    Indian Chopped Salad, 70

    Indian Grits with Vegetables, 30

    Mustardy Mashed Potatoes, 106

    Pan-Fried Silky Eggplant, 91

    Pepped-Up Cauliflower, 102

    Pickled Cucumber and Carrot Salad, 71

    Potato Raita with Cumin, 75

    Sautéed Coconut Chard, 105

    Shortcut Shrimp-Okra Curry, 134

Shredded Carrot Coconut Salad, 68

Smoky Eggplant Bharta, 107

A Spicy Bowl of Peas, 50

Tomato and Onion Koshimbeer, 68

Tomato Water, 55

Two-Greens Stew, 142

Whole Stuffed Okra, 101

Wholesome Spinach–Dal Soup, 57

Wilted Spinach with Red Chile, 110

Wok-Fried Potatoes, 104

vegetarian diet, 100, 139

w

"white" wheat flour, 29

whole lentils, 8

    Lentils with Curry Leaves, 143

Whole Stuffed Okra, 101

whole wheat flour, 8

Wholesome Spinach–Dal Soup, 57

Wilted Spinach with Red Chile, 110

Wok-Fried Potatoes, 104

y

yogurt, 38

    Banana Raita with Cayenne, 72

    Beet Raita with Cilantro, 72

    Butternut Squash Raita with Peanuts, 76

    Comforting Rice and Yogurt, 32

    Cucumber Raita with Curry Leaves, 74

    Curried Yogurt Pears, 140

    Indian Smoothie, 193

    Plain and Simple Raita, 77

    Potato Raita with Cumin, 75

    Salty Lassi, 187

    Sweet Lassi, 188

z

zucchini, 88